Local Matters

Local Matters

A Defence of Dooney's Café and Other Non-globalized Places, People, and Ideas

Brian Fawcett

Edited and with an introduction by Stan Persky

 NEW STAR BOOKS | *Vancouver* | 2003

New Star Books Ltd.
107 – 3477 Commercial Street
Vancouver, BC   V5N 4E8
www.NewStarBooks.com

Publication of this work is made possible by grants from the Canada
Council, the British Columbia Arts Council, and the Department of
Canadian Heritage Book Publishing Industry Development Program.

Le Conseil des Arts | The Canada Council
du Canada | for the Arts

BRITISH
COLUMBIA
ARTS COUNCIL

Printed and bound in Canada
First printing, October 2003

NATIONAL LIBRARY OF CANADA
CATALOGUING IN PUBLICATION

Fawcett, Brian, 1944–
Local matters / Brian Fawcett.
ISBN 1-55420-005-9
  I. Title.
S8561.A94L63 2003
C814´.54
C2003-905206-0

For Robin Blaser,
who introduced me to
the intellectual methods
used in this book.

Contents

Acknowledgements

Ian Adams, Leanna Crouch, Max Fawcett, Phinjo Gombu, David Mason, Rolf Maurer, T.F. Rigelhof, and as usual Graziano Marchese of Dooney's Café in Toronto. Early versions of many of these essays appeared on www.dooneyscafe.com. Others have appeared in *The Capilano Review*, *The Globe and Mail* and in *The Vancouver Review* (R.I.P.), in similarly embryonic formulations. "The Tides Are Caused by the Moon's Gravity, Not by Ours," was published as a chapbook by David Mason Books in 2001. "Marshall McLuhan Twenty Years Later" will someday appear in *At the Speed of Light There Is Only Illumination: A Reappraisal of Marshall McLuhan*, University of Ottawa Press.

Cosmopolitan Intelligence

An Introduction

THE FIRST TIME I HEARD Brian Fawcett read aloud was more than thirty years ago. I still remember the violence at the core of his story. It was called "Friends" and was a real-life folk tale about a brutal, profanity-laced fistfight in the back lots of Prince George, British Columbia, the Canadian town where Fawcett was born and raised. The story offered an account of a hopelessly outmatched, hysterically foul-mouthed young man fighting a stronger, more skilful, more emotionally balanced opponent. Each time the outmatched guy was bloodily decked, he pulled himself to his feet and, screaming expletives, mounted another futile charge. The friendship in the title was obviously ironic, but it also hinted at a deeper combative element in relationships, at least relationships in that particular place. From that story, circa 1970, to his most recent book, *Virtual Clearcut, or The Way Things Are in My Hometown* (Thomas Allen, 2003), Fawcett's writing advocates and defends the notion of a cosmopolitan intelligence applied to both local matters and global dilemmas.

The occasion for that initial encounter with Fawcett's work was a writers' meeting, one of a series of gatherings of mostly poets, held in the communal house where I lived in Vancouver. The young writers, in their twenties and thirties, who met regularly to read their work to each other included George Bowering, George Stanley, Gladys Hindmarch, Daphne Marlatt, Fawcett, myself, and a few others. I had first met Fawcett a couple of years earlier through my friend, the poet Robin Blaser, who was Fawcett's teacher at Simon

Fraser University. The writers who participated in those working sessions weren't a group in any formal sense, but we were animated by George Stanley's half-humorous notion of writing as Polyphonic Totalization, which he suitably announced in French (I think we were reading Jean-Paul Sartre's *Search for a Method* that year, hence the Frenchified theorizing). The serious idea underlying Stanley's clever phrase was to break through all genre and subject boundaries, to use any voice necessary (that was the polyphonic part), to write in a way that took account of the totality and fragmentation of the world, and to achieve a new and intense quality of authenticity. Well, impossible of course, but we produced a surprising amount of interesting writing.

One of those interesting pieces was Fawcett's story. What impressed me about the story was the rawness and intimacy of feeling that it conveyed. The story wasn't autobiographical except in the sense of Fawcett being an observer of the events of the narrative, yet at the same time I heard the protagonist's voice of obscene, unremitting rage as both a voice internalized by Fawcett as momentarily his own and, even more, as a normally unacknowledged element of the collective voice of the brutal, dark place that the story was representing.

Afterwards, I asked Fawcett, "Got any more like that one?" At the time, I was publishing a series of mimeographed books of all the writers I knew in Vancouver. I'd inherited the mimeograph machine used to print *Tish*, a Vancouver poetry magazine whose last issues I edited, installed it in the basement of our house, and, with the help of my friend Brian DeBeck, published Bowering's *Autobiology*, Marlatt's *Rings*, and my own *The Day*, among several others. When it turned out Fawcett did have "more like that one," I edited a selection of his early writing and became the publisher of his first book, *Friends* (Vancouver Community Press, 1971). In editing the present *Local Matters*, then, I come to the task familiar with the author's work.

For Fawcett, a lot of water has flowed under the bridges across the Nechako and Fraser rivers that run through Prince George since that first volume of stories and poems. Born there in 1944 into a large family engaged in local business, Fawcett grew up in the boom years of the mill town and himself worked in the forestry service. In the mid 1960s he moved to Vancouver, where he studied at Simon Fraser University, primarily with Robin Blaser and composer R. Murray Schafer, and after graduation worked for many years as an urban planner in the Greater Vancouver region while continuing to write poetry and edit two local literary magazines, *Iron* and *NMFG* (No Money From the Government). Some of the results of his studies with Blaser and other teachers turn up in *Local Matters* in the essay "How I Got a New American Education" (all essays cited in this introduction refer to material contained in this volume).

Some of Fawcett's "slapstick" work for Schafer is discussed in "The Tides Are Caused by the Moon's Gravity, Not by Ours." That's also the essay where he explains why, after publishing *The Opening* (1974), *Permanent Relationships* (1975), *Creatures of State* (1977), and *Aggressive Transport* (1982), he decided to declare a moratorium on publishing verse. My own reading of this crucial turn in his life as a writer is that there were basically three reasons for his decision. First, he believed it would be impossible to reach the readership he was seeking through poetry alone. Second, the kind of lyric poetry he was committed to writing suddenly seemed to him too self-involved, too dependent on self-expressiveness. Finally, and most important, ever since he was a teenager, Fawcett had been trying to write contemporary versions of the eighteenth-century poet Oliver Goldsmith's "The Deserted Village," with its famed couplet, "Ill fares the land, to hastening ills a prey, / Where wealth accumulates and men decay." Even though particular poems of Fawcett's like "Cottonwood Canyon," and others that I think of as "orchard elegies" in the spirit of Goldsmith, were sociopolitical in character, his notion of writing about "the most difficult subject matter I could locate," namely, "the largest and most urgent realities of the world I was in," as he says in "After *Cambodia*," demanded other forms.

What followed over the next decade or so was a remarkable series of books, beginning with *My Career with the Leafs* (1982), *Capital Tales*

(1984), and *The Secret Journal of Alexander Mackenzie* (1985). Although these volumes hinted at what was to come, they could be read as conventional and slightly unconventional short stories.

There then occurred one of those literary breakthrough moments that invariably mark the lives of all interesting writers. Fawcett tells the story in "After *Cambodia*" of deciding to investigate one of the most mysterious and horrifying stories of the last half of the twentieth century, the events that transpired in the country of Cambodia after the end of the Vietnam War in 1975. A revolution led by a political group known as the Khmer Rouge took place there, but instead of following the relatively pacific course of other communist revolutions in Southeast Asia, the one in Cambodia turned into a nightmarish, genocidal purification of the population in which the new regime slaughtered an enormous number of Cambodians in an attempt to purge, as Fawcett put it, all "memory and imagination." In writing about Cambodia, Fawcett found himself compelled to reexamine his own understanding of social catastrophes, especially as those understandings had been shaped in the course of his education by such works as Joseph Conrad's *Heart of Darkness* and the writings of Hannah Arendt on the subject of totalitarianism.

At the same time, Fawcett was writing a series of philosophical and often comic stories about experiences in contemporary society. The stories included odd, alienated episodes of eating unidentifiable fast food in interchangeable franchise restaurants in strip malls in the middle of nowhere, fantastic tales in which Marshall McLuhan and St. Paul discuss media on a screwball road to Damascus, and fictionalized analyses of how television chooses the angles by which to narrate human suffering. Although Fawcett only dimly recognized it at the time, they were stories about the effects of what we currently call "globalization."

Fawcett intuited that the globalization stories and the reflections on Cambodia were connected, but he didn't immediately see precisely how they related to each other. He took the disparate pieces of the manuscript to his publisher, Karl Siegler of Talonbooks in Vancouver, and with Siegler's perceptive help discovered that the structural solution that would turn the manuscript into a book was an experimental design, namely, to run the Cambodia investigation across the lower half of the pages, from beginning to end, and to put the stories on the top half of the pages. The result was *Cambodia: A Book for People Who Find Television Too Slow* (Talonbooks, 1986). It was a book that said that the threat to memory and imagination was as present in our own technologically charged civilization as it was elsewhere. It also said that the seeming immediacy, velocity, and truth of technologies like television (and eventually computers and the rest of the digitalia we now enjoy) were largely an illusion, as was the seeming plenitude generated by our economic cornucopia. It argued that real speed involved a density of understanding that could only be supplied by a cosmopolitan intelligence, that is, an intelligence at once specific and global. Those insights are further developed in *Local Matters* in such essays as "The Purpose of Paranoia," "Versus Virus," "Marshall McLuhan Twenty Years After," "Exile," and "Plenitude and Globalized Culture."

Cambodia was followed by *Public Eye: An Investigation into the Disappearance of the World* (Grove, 1989) and *Gender Wars* (Somerville House, 1994), work that drew on Fawcett's experiences as a teacher in federal maximum security prisons and his understanding of feminism. By the latter, I don't mean he had a merely academic interest in feminist theory, but rather that Fawcett strikes me as one of the few heterosexual men I know who has a genuine interest in how women experience themselves and the world. Together, the three books can be read, loosely, as a trilogy.

While *Cambodia* became something of a campus "cult classic," and though Fawcett's books were published in the U.S. and Britain as well as in Canada, he remains, in my view, a writer with far too few readers. Part of the inattention to his work can be explained by the vicissitudes of book publishing, marketing, and reviewing at a time when, to paraphrase Fawcett, the intellectual credibility of books has been diminished by the diminishment of intellectual credibility itself. Fawcett's writing — pugnacious, healthily suspicious, consistently interesting — is far removed not only from the self-expressive verse he abandoned, but also from most conventional Canadian literature (or CanLit) and other "prize-winning" writing in his homeland. As a writer whose work always strains genre boundaries, Fawcett is closer to such international authors as John Berger, V.S. Naipaul, Ryszard Kapuscinski, Primo Levi, and George Orwell than he is to most of his compatriots, excepting perhaps John Ralston Saul and a few other Canadian writers of literary non-fiction.

The 1990s, when he relocated to Toronto, was a fallow, but not unproductive, time for Fawcett. In addition to *Gender Wars*, he published a collection of essays, *Unusual Circumstances, Interesting Times* (New Star, 1991), to which this volume may be regarded as a follow-up. He is a serious enough gardener that he produced, in addition to backyard tomatoes and considerable landscaping advice for his Toronto neighbours, *The Compact Garden* (1992). He also surveyed the contemporary Canadian political and cultural scene in *The Disbeliever's Dictionary* (1997), with his usual disregard for conventional pieties. For most of the past decade, however, he was struggling with a book about three interconnected themes: the Bowron clearcut, a macroscopic logging smack-down near Prince George; the decline of his hometown in the context of globalism; and the relationships of the men of his own and the preceding generation. That book, *Virtual Clearcut; or, The Way Things Are in My Hometown* (2003), returns Fawcett to his primary concerns in literary non-fiction and is, in my view, the first important Canadian book of the new century.

Local Matters, which gathers up Fawcett's essays since *Unusual Circumstances*, can be read as a complement to *Virtual Clearcut*. The essays here are more broad-ranging and casual in terms of subject matter and approach. The pieces more or less naturally fall into two groups. The first group focuses on the relationship between the local — essays about matters as specific as the streets, cafés, and people in the Toronto neighbourhood where Fawcett lives — and the paranoia-inducing difficulties of conceptualizing globalism. In a sense, these essays are a turn on the old environmental slogan "Act locally, think globally." The second group of essays has as its central concern the relation of accurate language to the possibility of a humane polity, a theme whose most prominent recent proponent is George Orwell, a writer to whose work Fawcett's bears some resemblance. The essays in this group range from a discussion of "Why Writers Write" and "Writers and Responsibility" to specific literary assessments of such writers as Mordecai Richler and Jane Urquhart.

Most of the essays in this collection first appeared in earlier versions on the website www.dooneyscafe.com, an Internet location in which Fawcett and I have a hand. Though I tend to view the dooneyscafe website as similar to the mimeographed "little magazines" we both worked on in the 1960s and 70s, Fawcett takes the more activist position that dooneyscafe is "an alternate news service." In any case, we both agree that the sponsor of the website, the real-world Dooney's Café, located in Fawcett's Toronto neighbourhood, is a pretty hospitable place.

As in the concluding essay of *Local Matters*, "Cosmopolitans and the Definition of 'Good Family,'" a portrait of the Sikh intellectual Patwant Singh, a commitment to cosmopolitan intelligence presides over the entire collection.

What is cosmopolitan intelligence, and how is it distinguished from its counterparts? As implied by the etymology of its terms, it is a civic and literary intelligence that resides in worldly or universal polities, both actual and imagined. A universal polity is not necessarily a world city, much less a so-called world-class city. I've seen writers with cosmopolitan intelligence treat the small town or rural landscape in which they live as the centre of the universe. It is an intelligence that pays attention to the specificity of the local, while valuing and measuring that specificity in the context of larger entities in time and space, namely, history and the world. Cosmopolitan intelligence, like all thinking, has ideological commitments, but is demarcated from fundamentalisms and totalitarianisms in that it does not view phenomena through an ideological lens. Rather, it tests its beliefs through actual experiences. It proposes a concept of self which recognizes that self-expression is but the beginning, not the end, of individuality, and that its ethical measure is responsibility to others, the world, and language. The antagonist counterpart of cosmopolitan intelligence is parochial intelligence and, worse, forms of ignorance. By contrast, cosmopolitan intelligence is marked by curiosity, xenophilia, care for language, civility, and humour. Rather than belabour the point, let me invite you to a demonstration of cosmopolitan intelligence at work in the essays at hand.

Stan Persky
BERLIN
JULY 2003

Part One

Specificity

IN THE FALL OF 2000 I set up a web-based news service so Stan Persky and I could save a few trees while we recorded the things we were seeing, hearing, and thinking about the big globalizing marketplace both of us insist is called "the world." Stan had grown tired of putting up with the restrictive editorial bibles and word limits that are gradually reducing print journalism to the model of *USA Today*, and I needed to get my writing brain working again after I quit smoking. We had a second motive as well. Both of us — and most of the writers who interest us — often need long pieces to glean our teeming brains, and there are few venues left outside of *The New Yorker* that now print long essays. When they do, publication often comes several years after the piece is written, and the subject matter is stale or no longer of hot interest.

I was going to call the news service BSNS, which is an acronym for "Brian & Stan's News Service" or an abbreviation of the word "business." In my mind it would serve as both and anything else that fit. I wanted to call it a news service because what I had in mind was unconventional and non-denominational analysis and discourse, not the self-expressive "blog" writing that currently fills Internet sites, where writers mount websites so they can run on, stream-of-consciousness style, about whatever happens to be passing through their heads. Usually, it seems to me, what they write about is what they can see of their navels, or comes with so little structure and attention to research that it is virtually useless except to confirm already-held prejudices.

Around this time, Phinjo Gombu, a reporter for the *Toronto Star*, got interested and organized most of the technical elements of the site. He didn't want to write for it, but he liked the basic idea, and the technical challenge of building a website tweaked his curiosity. Then, just before BSNS launched, Graziano Marchese of Dooney's Café in Toronto offered to pay the cost of the server — about $300 a year — if I'd tie the website to the café, stick a small ad in the header, and write occasional stories on issues that came up in the neighbourhood. Since I spend most of my mornings at Dooney's, and it's a comfortable and unique-to-Toronto hangout for dozens of other writers and media renegades, his offer struck me as a near-perfect fit. Dooney's is the closest thing Toronto has to a literary café, and it ought to have a cyberspace equivalent. So I said, sure, all perfectly agreeable — free money is hard to find. A few weeks later we launched as www.dooneyscafe.com, and I started off to run it as I would have had it been named BSNS.

Within six months, dooneyscafe.com became as much Graziano's as mine and Stan's. Graziano began writing an occasional column on food — which meant he talked to me and I wrote down what he had to say. The service thus gained an unexpected view on the world, a much more local one than I originally intended. It became the cybernetic equivalent of the real-world café on Toronto's Bloor Street, which mixes a lookout on the local people, streets, and what happens between them with a cosmopolitan view of the larger world.

Despite the uneven quality of writing I've posted on dooneyscafe.com, it has made my world a sharper place to think in, and I'm grateful for that. I've come to a renewed understanding of the importance of careful observation of the community around me. The local is the only forum left where individuals can exercise compassion that isn't twisted by guilt at living so much higher on the hog than most of the planet's population.

The local, a.k.a. "the neighbourhood" — which I'll define as the geographical area a relatively healthy person can get around on foot — is also the arena for the most direct perception left to ordinary human beings. It will have topological features, unique weather, and enough familiar human faces to make you understand that you're not doomed to be a stranger in a strange land, or a mere consumer target in an entertainment or retail sales complex. Here in Toronto's downtown west, the topological boundaries are marked primarily by human constructions, except to the north, where the Pleistocene shores of Lake Ontario are visible, a ridge atop which sits the fairyland castle of Casa Loma and Wychwood Park, where Marshall McLuhan lived. Queen Street West marks the south boundary. It is now the city's most fashionable street for both retail and cultural avant-garde experiences and overflows with funky boutiques and funkier restaurants I rarely visit but faithfully point out to out-of-town visitors.

To the east, the boundary is, depending how much you like walking, the University of Toronto, the Ontario Legislature at Queen's Park, and hospital-lined University Avenue with its procession of deservedly ignored public sculptures. Yonge Street lies a little farther east, where you can see, at Bloor and Yonge, the transformation of Canada's retail sector into a franchise strip mall. Just north of the intersection, thought of by easterners as the centre of Canada, is the building that once housed Albert Britnell Books, which was the country's oldest bookstore until a Chapters and an Indigo superstore strangled it. It is now a Starbucks outlet. Next door is a Tim Hortons, a Canadian doughnut company started by a chronically drunk Toronto Maple Leafs defenceman and now owned by an American named Wendy. Between those two environments lies the cultural space the corporate sector would like everyone to inhabit. East again, for serious athletes, is the Don Valley, with its polluted stream, the impassable-on-foot parkway, and the Bloor Viaduct, which has just been suicide-proofed to prevent the distraught from splattering themselves on the parkway pavement.

The west boundary is defined more by taste and ethnicities. I don't venture far that way unless I'm heading out of town or going to Roncesvalles Avenue to shop at the Polish delicatessens there. But west along Bloor Street lie some of the city's most extreme microneighbourhoods: the four blocks of Little Korea west of

Bathurst, then several blocks of Somalis, Ethiopians, and Latinos pushed west by the Koreans. After that, ethnic distinctions blend back into the Portuguese and Italian majority, and the streets are hard to characterize except as funky or run-down until the intersection of Bloor and Dundas. To the south lies Roncesvalles, which is the cultural locus for the city's 190,000 Poles, a surprising number of whom are recent arrivals — refugees from the post-Soviet mess. Farther west along Bloor begins the gentrification of High Park and High Park Village, which retains an Eastern European flavour despite the heftier incomes of its residents.

I've never liked walking, so my real neighbourhood consists of the old Hungarian area from Bathurst east to Spadina on Bloor Street, and College Street, which is my centre and south boundary all at once, between Bathurst and Ossington, which is about ten blocks to the west. I walked my daughter along these streets while she was an infant, first football-style in the crook of my arm, then in a backpack (inside which she munched on a bread stick from Riviera Bakery), then later on my shoulders, farther west, for Sicilian ice cream. Now we walk hand in hand, she chattering merrily about how many songs her boyfriends can sing. As things sit, her favourite contemporary knows just two songs — "Oh Canada" and the refrain from *Bob the Builder* — whereas I stand supreme, no doubt temporarily, as the hundred-song'd boyfriend. I know many of the shopkeepers we pass by name. My daughter knows more, the result of spending the year when she was three in the company of a Mary Poppins nanny we hired, a woman who liked to spend her afternoons drinking cappuccino and chatting with anyone able to speak any one of her five languages.

The weather in our neighbourhood is distinctive, too. Like the microclimates across southern Ontario, ours is extreme, but the proximity to Lake Ontario makes it comparatively civilized without sacrificing any of its entertaining drama. In the long Ontario winters, downtown Toronto is usually two to three degrees centigrade warmer than its suburbs, which often spares us from the winter white-outs that regularly scramble the freeways and occasionally close the airport. In summer the city is a few degrees cooler than the suburbs due to the breezes off the lake, which make the steamy heat bearable.

The dominant ethnicity of this neighbourhood is Italian, even though Italians no longer outnumber the Portuguese, Chinese, or Anglos. Greater Toronto has almost 600,000 Italians, the majority of whom came from Calabria in the decades after the Second World War. They're confident and competently urbanite here, and although many from the first generation never learned to speak English fluently, they're friendly and welcoming, and they run the place well. I'm happy among them, despite not being able to speak Italian, which my neighbours insist would be of little use in deciphering the Calabrian dialect, and feel gratefully at home.

The specifics of these changing but peaceful streets have driven home something I've been reluctant to understand as a primary fact of existence. I've been aware for a long time that I have a very lucky life, but I wasn't willing to admit that people in other parts of the world are justified in resenting those of us who live as well as I do. We are — North Americans and most Europeans — by the sheer volume of our consumption, a threat to everyone else's future and to *their* quality of life.

That's why, among other things, the righteous rage of George W. Bush's war against terrorism is at once slightly shameful and disingenuous. We know, deep down, the reason for the al-Qaeda attacks on the World Trade Center. They were the manifestation of a long-stewed mixture of rancour, envy, and fear. I'm not suggesting that the attacks were justified. Rather, they're *understandable* if we refuse to lie to ourselves, and no thoughtful Westerner should respond to their violence with mere indignation and righteous rage. The currents of unease the attacks have inspired need to be examined without shrouding them in the fog of guilt or the false certainties of countering fundamentalisms. The only way to do that is to examine the specific textures of local life and to read its landscapes and civilities against those of people living in, say, Kabul or Basra or Kigali. I have a fairly simple first principle that I apply here: I haven't had to worry about being beaten to death because my writing has offended a dictator's psychopathic son, and my wife hasn't had to trade in her television job to cower under a suffocating blue tablecloth. So far, so good. Then I start in on the specifics.

My neighbourhood tailor, Paul, has a shop at 673 Bathurst Street, just south of Harbord Street, called Madelaine Tailors. He refuses to charge for altering my daughter's clothes. This is hardly a crime, but he charges so little for the other work he does for us that it feels like I'm stealing from him. He has an explanation for the no-charge policy. He wants to build up his customer base for the next generation.

Paul, whose last name I've been unable to uncover because he insists that I call him by his Christian name, is one of those treasures that every city neighbourhood must have. He's Eastern European, probably Hungarian, appears to be in his late seventies, and his health isn't always sound. Both his accent and his manners are elegant enough to make conversation with him a pleasure, but there are several topics that are closed. I can't get him to talk about his age, or how long he's been there, because he doesn't entertain personal questions. When you're in his shop he's interested in you, not himself, and in the quality of the clothing you bring in, the latter of which he'll discuss in detail if you're interested, and he's eloquent about materials and workmanship alike.

Judging from his shop and the machines he uses, he's been in business a very long time and I'm pretty sure he no longer needs to work. But he clearly loves making and repairing clothing, and the more difficult the challenge you bring in, the more cheerful and loquacious he becomes. A few months ago I brought him an expensive jacket that had become too small to wear because I'd gained weight after I quit smoking. By opening every seam in the jacket, he reproduced it a full size larger. He charged me less than $20 when I'd have happily paid at least $100, and I had to haggle with him for ten minutes before he'd agree to take $30. My wife, Leanna, has had a half-dozen similar experiences with him because we've since gone out of our way to find projects for him to work on. We haven't done this because we're cheapskates trying to save money by recycling old clothes, but because we've wanted to give him something to exercise his remarkable skills upon. There's a certain urgency to this because there's no telling how long we'll have him around. I'd dearly love my daughter to be one of his next-generation customers, but the odds are long because old people die, even if they are good people like Paul.

We lost one of those old, good people recently when Frank's Garage at 283 Harbord closed. The news of the closing, followed within days by news of the owner's death, went around the neighbourhood swiftly because Frank — another Eastern European in his seventies — and his garage were a much-appreciated neighbourhood amenity. He wasn't the city's best auto mechanic, but he was its most honest. If you came in with a mechanical problem, he'd often puzzle over it for hours. If he couldn't fix it, he didn't charge you for his time. When he did fix something, his prices were always reasonable, and if you brought in a job he knew he couldn't do as well as another garage, he'd tell you exactly which one to take it to and what to expect.

Frank kept the garage open until a month before he died. Toward the end, the tentativeness of his step and his periodic absences told you he wasn't well, even though he never spoke about it and was as cheerful and courteous as ever. He closed down his business quietly and without fanfare, exactly as he did his life, which I'm sure he'd lived the same way he ran the garage.

I never had a personal conversation with Frank. Like Paul the tailor, he always addressed me formally — as "Mr. Fawcett" — even though I called him "Frank," like everybody else did. We talked about my Honda Accord, which he was fond of because it is fourteen years old and still has less than 100,000 kilometres on the odometer. Each time I brought it in, which wasn't often, he'd mention what a good car it was and then warn me not to sell it. One time when I brought it in for a spring tune-up, he sent me away. He'd checked the oil and found it clean, let it idle in the shop for a few minutes, and when I came back he told me it didn't need the tune-up and that I shouldn't waste my money. That was his way of taking his work personally. I don't imagine he left a great fortune behind, running a business that way, but he left a small part of the world better off than he'd found it, along with a sizable group of mourners who think the neighbourhood is a less sweet place now that he's not there.

Meanwhile, I've acquired new neighbours across the street on Euclid Avenue. They're vegan lawyers with two large dogs that suffer from "separation anxieties," which the lawyers admit is going to translate into a lot of loud daytime barking. The previous owner of the house, Alfie, had lived there since 1957, and he was the most house-proud homeowner on the block. His house was fully renovated — Italian style — and immaculately kept up. He left the house so spotless the newcomers said they could have eaten off the floors, and he clearly expected them to move into the place and live happily ever after without changing a thing.

Fat chance. The first of five dumpsters appeared the day after the lawyers gained possession, and it was a jumbo. The metal canopy over the front porch disappeared into it within the first hour, and the workmen went after the beige vinyl trim on the upper part of the house soon after, while another set of workmen wheelbarrowed away the white ceramic kitchen floor Alfie left them to eat off. Subsequent dumpsters carted off the rest of the kitchen, the recently installed three-quarter-inch oak floors from the living room, and almost all the plaster in the house. The second-floor front bedroom disappeared to make an interior courtyard and a home legal library, which now has a Mac G4 turned on twenty-four hours a day. The lawyers aren't finished renovating, and by the time they're done it will be impossible to tell that Alfie ever lived there.

I'm sorry to see Alfie leave. He was a good, perpetually cheerful if overly talkative, neighbour. The bags of smelts he distributed each spring were a major boost to our quality of life, as was the three-storey display of white Christmas lights he put up each December. The good taste of the lawyers will no doubt jack up house prices along the street a little more, but I'd rather have Alfie's free smelts and Christmas lights.

The darkest cloud on this horizon — and a backhanded testimony to the importance of specificity — appeared in our mailbox a few weeks ago. It was almost certainly delivered by a neighbour who'd seen our orange tabby standing around — and likely caterwauling — on our front porch. It was a three-page circular concerning the proper supervision of felines, with some added highlighting and circling of relevant paragraphs. One highlighted sentence asked us to write to our council member requesting that new legislation be passed to make sterilizing all domestic cats mandatory. Another suggested that all cats should be kept inside because of the terrible things that can happen to them, and warned us that if our cat relieved itself in a neighbour's yard, Animal Services could pick him up and presumably execute him. One full page of the circular provided a graphic description of how a single pair of breeding cats can produce 80 million kittens in ten years.

Our cat happens to be eighteen years old, and he was sterilized at six months. Leanna has had this animal much longer than she's had me, actually. She picked him from a Humane Society cage because she thought he was lonely, and because the way he was hanging from the wire mesh of his holding cage, howling, looked cute. He spent the first thirteen years of his life indoors, and he wasn't happy about it. He occupied most of his hours complaining vocally about his overprotected life and trying to escape. Long before I arrived, she had his front claws removed. That sounds cruel, but he treated all curtains, windowsills, and doors as impediments to his freedom and took a perverse joy in shredding them. Whenever he managed to escape, he also shredded whatever fools Leanna dragooned into aiding in the recapture. Locating him once he was out was never difficult. The rescuers simply had to locate the nearest fellow feline, which he would be trying to exterminate.

This cat was (and remains) a little cracked, in other words. He was lonely at the Humane Society as a kitten because he'd had to be separated from his littermates. Right from the beginning, I guess, he's been a social Darwinist. In his mind it was either him or his brothers and sisters, and from there it got more extreme. Having his claws removed may have spared a few curtains and the woodwork, but it didn't help those who had to recapture him after an escape, and it was murder on other cats. He quickly figured out that front claws are mostly ornaments useful for threatening one's enemies, that his hind claws could do more damage, and that he had a mouthful of very sharp teeth. With outdoor humans and other cats he skipped the formalities and simply attacked, a technique that served him well in cat fights and prolonged more than one escape.

When we moved to the house we now live in during the spring of 1997, I liberated him, even though I knew there was some chance that we'd lose him. He wasn't traffic-wise, and the next-door neighbour kept three large tomcats he'd rescued from Kensington Market, one of which weighed at least twenty pounds and had lost both ears and one eye in fights. But there was nothing to worry about. Our cat figured out how to cross the street safely in the first few hours, and once he knew he could go outside whenever he felt the urge, he calmed down, slightly. When he wasn't feeling calm, his no-preliminaries approach to feline socialization worked fine. Then one evening about a month after I let him go feral, I looked over the edge of the porch and found him and the three nasties from next door in a circle commune, all four facing one another with their paws tucked under their bodies, which is the feline signal of peaceful intentions.

Today, he's a happy animal. He's still psychotic, but he's no danger to people unless they try to pet him for longer than ten or fifteen seconds. He still goes out, complains loudly at the door if he's left out longer than he likes, and occasionally I'll find him trotting along with the dog and me on our late evening walks — although he probably imagines that he's stalking us. He's living pretty much his self-absorbed, noisy idea of the good life, even if this isn't always easy for self-absorbed human beings to recognize.

His good life isn't good enough for that circular-distributing well-intentioned busybody. She — or he — thinks my cat is about to turn into 80 million kittens. Like all people who think the creatures around them are in need of supervision, the busybody is paying more attention to what they'd like to see — or not see — than to what's actually there. In this case what he/she is trying to supervise is an old cat who poops indoors, yowls because he likes the sound of his own voice, and isn't afraid of anything because he's crazy. He's not planning to mate with every female cat in a two-hundred-mile radius, nor will he fill the neighbour's yard with microbe-infested poo.

Which brings us back to specificity, and to busybodies, of which my part of the world has far too many. They want to ban everything they even suspect could impinge on their safety and their privacy, and they want to supervise everything and everyone else that might cross the perimeters they've set up. That's a problem, in my mind.

It's not merely that today's strain of busybody happens to irritate me. It has to do with the notions of community they restrict us to. Communities designed to service the narcissisms or obsessions of their individual members aren't viable or humane, nor are groups that define themselves by excluding other communities or individuals or by wanting to impose their obsessive compulsions on them. These are definitions for gang warfare and will result in long-term social lunacy: Rwanda, or the former Yugoslavia. They aren't a relevant response to the unapologetic complexity of the twenty-first century.

To make any community functional — which is to say infra- and extra-relationally relevant — requires two basic intentions. Both of them are generous and inclusive. One is a willingness to see things as they present themselves in fine detail — as in, my cat is well-groomed, skinny, and unscarred, and the two little circles under his tail aren't puffed out and stinky, so leave him alone. The second intention is a generous curiosity about how the fine details of communal life can and do intertwine with one's own. My busybody neighbour, ergo, should have taken the time to stop, pet my cat, and make a quick inspection. That would have been met with ten seconds of civility before the cat sank his yellowing fangs into the back of the busybody's hand. After that, real-world specifics would have reigned, as they should.

This sort of neurotic misapprehension of specificity is endemic these days and is the product, I suspect, of globalism's subtle but pervasive assault on the perimeters of individual consciousness. Moral conscience is a fine thing, but it raises little effective defence against that assault. A more generous curiosity, fuelled by specificity — the kind embodied by people like Paul or Frank or Alfie — may be the most effective tool in the struggle against globalism and the always lowering common denominators it imposes. People need to insist on being where they are, and they need to pay closer attention to people and things that are specific and original. This means rejecting the generic as, at best, second-rate. That's often as simple a matter as giving value to those things that globalism can't, and doesn't want to, manufacture or duplicate.

The Tides Are Caused by the Moon's Gravity, Not by Ours

A Personal Essay on the Future of Poetry

IN THE EARLY 1980s, after fifteen years of publishing reasonably subtle and technically elaborate lyric poems in magazines and books that no one read, I woke up one morning to the unpleasant recognition that publishing my lyric poetry in the late twentieth century was equivalent to playing with my penis on a busy street corner — and having everyone ignore me. The insight was humiliating enough that I decided to stop publishing my verse and to stop giving public readings of it. The only poems I've since allowed into print were several I let some friends publish a few years ago. I did it without expecting to be paid in money or attention. I was neither disappointed nor surprised when publication and non-publication met with the same response.

There is nothing tragic here. Ceasing to publish verse didn't profoundly affect the quality of my life, spiritual or otherwise. My heart didn't break, the Muses didn't torment my sleep, nor did I slip off my edge of the so-called real world because I stopped mumbling short-line sentences to small, close-to-comatose audiences. Actually, it was more like coming up with the right insight at the right time, although I ought to admit the insight had been waving its hands in my face for years, trying to attract my attention.

Some luck with technology made things easier for me. Word processors were becoming common around 1980, and I had enough money to buy one. When I stopped being a poet, I was able to make a relatively smooth transition to being a *writer*, one who produced big, long sentences that turned into paragraphs and pages of prose rather easily. Soon I was writing heavily revised books, some of it fiction, but more often the metaphor-laced philosophical speculations and cultural or political commentary that had always been my true passion. I had a lot in my mind, and a lot on it. Ceasing to publish poems opened up the length, breadth, and depths of the world to write about, and I wrote energetically and compulsively. For a decade I continued to *write* verse in private, but in steadily decreasing quantities and with a gradual but relentless decay in the attentions that provoke occasional verse. I kept thinking about that street corner, I guess.

A year or so after I stopped publishing verse, somewhere near the mid 1980s, I accepted an invitation from Ottawa troublemaker and editor John Metcalf to write an essay for one of his critical anthologies about exactly why I'd stopped publishing verse. I wrote three thousand words on my Apple II+ within a few hours of Metcalf's invitation, then rethought and rejigged it fifteen or twenty times. Before long I had a version of my street-corner insight dressed up in the ideas that had been swirling around it, and I'd become a writer who, for the first time, felt productive rather than merely sensitive.

The essay started by suggesting that verse has become a technically obsolete art form that new media have recently rendered culturally and cognitively incomprehensible to most people. From there I went a long way out of my way to dis both the publishing apparatus behind its publication in Canada and the self-expression industry that has built itself around verse as the products of feckless neurotics, incompetent exhibitionists, lazy grant-sucking publishers, and other cyber-capitalist opiates too numerous and loathsome to name.

But I wasn't *completely* bloody-minded in my condemnations. I made what felt like a slightly cute distinction between verse-making and poetry, then announced that I believed that poetry remained "the most profound manifestation of human imagination that exists, and . . . one of the most powerful tools human intelligence has ever devised — the act from which nearly all civilized behaviors have derived."

The polemical altitude I reached with that zinger made me feel giddy, but I wanted to go higher before I sent everything crashing down to the level of common sense. So I shifted ground, rustled my priestly cassock, rubbed my hands along the edges of the pulpit, and murmured that I couldn't "imagine living a life that does not have poetry somewhere near its centre." After adding that fewer people now read poetry than write it and that publication has become either a sour academic sport or a semi-obligatory response to the availability of government publishing subsidies, I concluded that I couldn't see any acceptable reason for continuing to publish verse.

I'd plunged one foot recklessly far into what felt like sticky if minor truths, and so I thought, well, why not see how much deeper it is to the logical conclusions at the base of those truths? I allowed that I was intellectually embarrassed by the lack of rigour in contemporary verse manufacture, including my own, and that I wanted to do a kind of writing that had some degree of affective influence on the world, indirect or direct. Until I could produce the kind of verse in which the investigative rather than the self-revelatory elements were in the forefront, I said, I'd desist from further public waste of paper and public attention and would inflict no more unwanted poesy on sleepy audiences.

But it wasn't until I said I was going to take a ten-year rain check on the business of *publishing* poetry, and then made a deadly serious proposition that other poets do likewise, that I got myself into serious trouble. The business I was making sport of, you see, really *is* a business, within which moderately lucrative and very secure teaching careers can be wrought, money made, and absurd quantities of over-distilled self-regard bottled for the decline into silence. Entrepreneurs, it turns out, leave their silver trails across the walls and ceilings of the temples of contemporary verse, just as they do in the real world. So when the essay was published, "the Biz" disappeared me. I can't recall a single publishing poet who has acknowledged the existence of that essay since it was published, and only one or two academics who have gone beyond rolling their eyes and tsk-tsking me about it.

I got on with my writing life. I'd pretty much mined out my youthful lyric vein anyway, and had already begun the process of learning that human life is not quite about my feelings — and that the "I" part of it was the one I have the least shot at articulating accurately. The years started passing, swiftly and pretty happily, and I ended up in different parts of the human and literary universes.

Then, a few months ago, a likable young magazine editor in Vancouver asked me to send him something on a magazine I'd written for and helped to edit while I was at university in the late 1960s and early 1970s. He wanted me to write something about the ethos of the magazine, about writing and editing in general, and specifically about what elements of writing and literature I'd changed my mind about over thirty years.

I've never archived my past diligently, so I had to ask the editor for several back issues of the magazine. He sent them on, and when I read them through I was pleasantly surprised. The writing was slightly better than I remembered it: intense, self-dramatizing, but technically quite competent. It was also obliviously sophomoric — as it should have been. The poems I'd written for it were as obliviously sophomoric as any of the others. Or were they more so?

I'd been in my late twenties when I wrote those poems, and it hadn't been a happy time for me. I'd begun to get a dark inkling that my first wife and I might not make it, and neither would a lot of other things that had once seemed pure and sure. This quite naturally got into the poems I wrote, and it made them embarrassingly personal and coded, whiny elegiacs of how hard and complicated adult life was. I should have been making thorough and precise registrations of the things around me, or trying to figure out what I might be able to do to save my marriage and make my life satisfying and interesting. Alas, I was more compelled by the Virgilian gloom I detected at the edges of those things, and I couldn't see that most of it was emanating from inside my own dopey head.

One of the poems I published in the magazine, a lament that draped itself across its pages in a William Carlos Williams-style graphic layout, particularly interested me. It was titled, rather unhelpfully for anyone but its author, "Pachena Bay." I'd written it after making a trip to the west coast of Vancouver Island in the spring of 1970. The poem seemed content (as I was in those days) to ward off the depressing relentlessness of adult life with a humour-less sort of cosmological cynicism — we may be fucked up, but so is the universe, etc. The poem mooned about the observed peculiari-ties of the coastal light after twilight, and about the sheer number and brilliance of stars, which it pronounced, in a half-cooked pun on its West Coast setting, the "end of the known world." From that static Apocalypse, it perceived "the white snarl of the breakers / the lip / curling in the roar of / a heavenly smile. / To have love / slip away / always / slip away."

The reason the poem interested me after thirty years was that the "slipping away" references recalled, instead of Virgilian gloom, a piece of slapstick that occurred while I was at the location for which the poem is titled. I'd been both the main actor and the victim of the slapstick, which, while it involved some slipping, had its main items coming at me rather than receding into poetical gloom. The physical comedy of the slapstick didn't get into the poem, naturally. If it had, and if I'd been willing to engage it as content, it might have pro-voked some useful insights. It might also have provided me with a solution to the compositional dilemma that, even then, lyric poetry was beginning to present, but that's a subject I'll reserve until I've told the story.

I was out on the west coast of Vancouver Island to record some live surf for a quadraphonic musical composition R. Murray Schafer was allowing Bruce Davis and me to help him construct in the elec-tronic music studio at Simon Fraser University. To make the record-ings, Schafer had entrusted to my care two state-of-the-art Uher portable reel-to-reel stereo tape recorders. The Uhers were good machines, but by today's standards cumbersome and heavy, using five-inch reels of quarter-inch tape and a raft of now-obsolete recording subsystems that can today be fitted inside a ballpoint pen. The Uhers were also fantastically expensive to buy — about $3,000 each, if I recall correctly.

I'd chosen Pachena Bay for the recording location because I'd been there before and had heard something attractive in the har-monics of the surf. The bay's beach wasn't a spectacular or very large one, little more than a three- or four-hundred-metre stretch of sand

and gravel a few kilometres south of Barkley Sound and Bamfield. A more conventional choice would have been to go farther north to the better-known Tofino beaches and hang out with the hippies. But Pachena was closer to Vancouver, it had a foreshore sufficiently deep for my dimly conceived purposes, and it was angled so that parts of it were sheltered enough from the ocean winds to make clean recordings possible. It was also certain to be clear of possible witnesses in case I screwed up.

I arrived on site late in the afternoon of a cold spring day and immediately headed for the water to satisfy my curiosity about the wave harmonics. I'd heard ocean waves in other places, of course, but what I remembered about the surf here was a certain "tambourine" quality — a pleasant rustling complexity at the base of the harmonic. It didn't take long to figure out the most likely source of it. For fifty to seventy-five metres of the foreshore from low tide point, the middle portion of the beach was a spongy mix of half-inch gravel and shells, mostly littleneck clam shells mixed with some giant mussel, razor clam, and what appeared to be oyster shells — all of which became percussive in an active tide. Satisfied, I returned to the car and unpacked my camping gear. I carried it to a log just beyond the limit of the beach sand. The log offered some shelter from the wind, and I built a driftwood lean-to onto it, tying a plastic tarp I'd brought over the frame. Then I collected enough wood for a cooking fire and a chilly evening in a sleeping bag, and began to unpack my recording equipment.

The tide book I'd brought told me that low tide was going to coincide roughly with sunset, and well before the light began to fade I had my two machines set up on a large log that had marooned itself parallel to the waterline midway up the foreshore. With four channels to record, the setup was quite complicated. I taped four heavy and very expensive microphones onto adapted camera tripods a few feet in front of my log, wound the cords through the straps on the Uhers, and pushed the jacks into the recording slots of the machines. Then I climbed up onto the log to watch the sun slip below the horizon and the sea begin its advance up the foreshore — and, not incidentally, to contemplate my existentially outcast fate. I'd calculated that I should be able to record about ten to fifteen minutes of acceptable ambiance before the incoming tide forced me to dismantle the equipment and retreat thirty metres up the beach to the next log, where I would repeat the recording.

My setup and plan weren't terrible, but each had fatal flaws. As a preface, shortly after I arrived, I dropped my only flashlight into a tide pool. Maybe I dropped it because I was distracted by the poetic urge to Bewail my Outcast Fate, as my poem suggests, but the only thought I can remember having when I realized the flashlight was taking on water was "Oh shit." I repeated that imprecation when the sun sank below the horizon more quickly than I'd expected and the billions of stars overhead didn't brighten the beach in any way useful to a guy trying to operate twin stereo tape recorders from a log.

The most serious flaw was the one I didn't see at all. The stretch of foreshore where I'd set up shop was flatter than I'd realized, and the tide snaked up it more rapidly than I was prepared for. Cold, salty water was soon bumping aggressively against my log, which instantly demonstrated that it wasn't as stable as I'd assumed. I got just three safe minutes to make my recordings instead of fifteen. Before I could pack up and move to the higher log — perhaps this was when I paused to notice the White Snarl of the Breakers, or Love Slipping Away — the waves undermined one of the microphone tripods. I lunged to catch it as it teetered toward the salt water, my arm caught the strap of the Uher it was plugged into, and both the mike and the Uher made a brief but terminal visit to Davy Jones's locker.

I did rescue the other three microphones and the second Uher, and I even regrouped to record almost twenty minutes of perfectly usable surf ambiance later that evening. I did it by standing in the bone-chilling seawater up to my knees with the surviving tape recorder slung across my shoulders and two of the microphones held at arm's length, still on their tripods, to obtain the maximum stereo effect. I half-rescued myself from a major fuck-up, in other words — half-fixed a bad situation I'd created through my own stupidity and inattention.

Thirty years later, I can see that this was a seminal moment in my life, one in which I'd acted characteristically. That little piece of slap-stick-on-the-beach was me, then and today. I also note that as a *writer*, I failed the moment miserably. I wrote only a sappy nature poem about how many stars there are once you get clear of the cities, and how lonely and confusing it is to be in your late twenties and attracted to every female you encounter who doesn't have a horde of nose warts worthy of the Wicked Witch of the West. Those insights weren't even news to me at the time, so why was I recording — and then, for god's sake, publishing — them instead of delivering the deliciously revealing piece of slapstick I'd performed with the Uhers and the Pachena Bay tide?

The insights I might have gleaned from the slapstick had pro-found (and for me, permanently relevant) implications. They are, from the specific to the general:

(1) If one is going out into the big world to make the world's first quadraphonic audio taping of surf, one ought to take some competent technicians along if one doesn't want to risk (a) cata-strophic failure and (b) the destruction of expensive equipment.
(2) The tides are caused by the moon's gravity, not by ours.
(3) Don't run in the surf if you're not prepared to get wet.
(4) Don't be stargazing unless you're in a warm, dry location.
(5) There is more safety in foresight and planning than in trusting to technology.

In 1970, such ostensibly technical and mundane insights didn't seem like something I could transform into poetry, while chewing on the cosmic and/or human scenery did. Too bad. If I'd pursued some of the practical messages that episode tried to deliver to my teeming brain, I might have produced a piece of readable writing. Even if I hadn't, working the practicalities would have given me more peace of mind than my lofty visions of the sea and stars did. For years after this disaster, you see, I felt bad about ruining the Uher, even though, to his credit, Schafer himself had been more amused than angry when I told him what I'd done. It's possible that he already understood how much more valuable insight and innovation are than state-of-the-art technology. Still, I don't recall him sending me on any more missions that risked valuable equipment. Maybe he decided that the only insights I was capable of appropriating then were the kind I was recording in my poems.

There was more. A few weeks later, Schafer, Davis, and I did use what I brought back from Pachena Bay for our quadraphonic composition. We dubbed my quarter-inch half-track tape and then delayed the two dubbed tracks a half second each to create a harmonized wave roll in glorious quadraphonic sound. This time I *did* get the implicit lesson: In the electronic media, it is what people accept as authentic that matters, not how the authenticity is produced.

Too bad it didn't occur to me to apply this to writing poetry or to my personal life, because it pointed straight at my best talents as a writer and as a human being. I was and remain a late-in-the-game fabricator of apparently inappropriate and disparate materials, a rectifier — partially and perhaps inexactly — of major foul-ups, fuckups, errors-in-judgment, slapstick mistakes, and so forth. I don't foresee the future any better than John Naismith, Charles Olson, or NORAD and CNN, but then art and artists are with us to let us know what's on the end of those forks we're putting in our mouths, not to predict the future. What art — alone of all the human mental crafts — does well is what I managed to do that day: read a messy situation and act on it accurately enough to bring some small part of it, alive, laughing, and whole, through to the next episodes in the ongoing fuck-up called the human condition. For posterity or for itself or for the sheer joy of the human dance. Doesn't matter.

So if I was, in my late twenties, too self-involved to write competent poetry, and in my late thirties not resourceful enough to solve the compositional and philosophical weaknesses that made my nominally accomplished lyric verse embarrassing to me, why am I now, well into my fifties, digging through this musty bone-yard and trying to repress a sense of regret and loss? In turning my back on verse, and the poetry subculture Biz around it, did I give up the essential tools of poetry — or anything else that is useful to understanding the world?

There don't seem to be easy answers to those questions. They aren't rhetorical. They're so alive and permeable, in fact, that it is pointless to approach them frontally. So let me go back to the questions the magazine editor asked that touched this off, and see if *they* offer an environment I can think in. These were his questions: Do I see writing differently than I did in 1970? If I do, what are the important differences?

The answer to the editor's first question is a firm yes. My understanding of what writing and writers can (and ought to) achieve within a human society has changed. During my lifetime, writers and writing have been supplanted as the dominant interpreter of human values by the more corporate and less privately demanding media of television, film, and popular music, and I can hardly deny the effect of this without being a fool. One can now become an "important" writer and be without any significant influence.

Given that fundamental alteration, it remains possible to say that good writing is still valuable because it permits us to treat complex subject matters with conceptual precision and thus enhances our ability to think accurate, complex thoughts and to communicate them to others. More broadly, a society needs to be able to articulate complexities if it is to avoid social and interpersonal violence as problem-solving devices. Beyond that, clear language, widely employed, is a first-line tool for any human grouping that aspires to be just and healthily democratic.

Beneath the changes brought on by the new media, clear language — specifically metaphor and rhetoric — remains the first instrument of both public and private clarity. Properly considered in isolation from its waning aesthetic value, poetry (if not verse and the Biz) has always acted as the janitorial service for metaphor and rhetoric, both of which require high degrees of maintenance to protect their vitality and their precision. Absurd as it may now sound, the virtues of a poet's pursuit may be more important than the bean counter's virtues that obsess today's private and public sectors.

All of these latter things I would have agreed with in 1970 if I'd recognized their presence. But I've also changed my mind about the role the self plays in the operation of poetry, and the degree to which sublimating — or even suppressing — the self is necessary to achieve relevant accuracy in the use of poetic language. My change of mind is partly a consequence of having my testosterone levels drop low enough that I can occasionally think through something without erotic and biomission intrusions fogging up my glasses. It is also partly the product of recognizing that there are no stable and reliable pathways from the self into the world. In 1970 I believed that the road to poetic accuracy ran right through the most rubble-littered intersections of the self. That was the fatuous *Zeitgeist* of the 70s: Any world cleanup must be preceded by spiritual self-cleansing. Now I understand that it is the world that creates the paths, not the self, and that unrestrained self-determination might be the greatest danger to human survival.

Twentieth-century history intrudes here, and mightily. Lyric poetry, as we who write in English know it and practise it, is the product of the Great War of 1914–1918. In the course of placing 60 million men of breeding age into a hell of mud, steel, and high explosives, and then setting them to murder and maim one another, the ruling classes of the era unwittingly subjected the young of their educated classes to stresses — collective misery without satisfactory ritual solidarities, massive numbers of premature and pointless deaths, and a cognitive culture that valorized meditation under extreme and unreasonable physical conditions — that could only be comprehended and articulated through lyric devices. The British, more than any other combatant nation, seem to have gone out of their way to exterminate an entire generation of their well-educated and articulate young men this way. They killed most of them, but not before the young men glimpsed the world in ways that previous generations of wealthy and privileged men had been sheltered from.

For anyone who sets out to study the human effects of the Great War upon those who fought it or were near to it, it is almost impossible to ignore how ubiquitous the writing of verse became among educated young officers — who, incidentally, suffered the highest casualty percentage of any demographic group that fought in the war. They wrote poems, these young men, and they were blown up and machine-gunned and bayoneted, and they wrote more poems and were gassed and shell-shocked into catatonia or shivering incoherence. And still they wrote poems. Most of the poems disappeared with the dead poets, the intellectual portion of the 50 to 65 percent of men who went to war and were simply lost in the barbarism that ensued, men without graves, poems without distinction, lives without dignity or value except as attritional ciphers in a blundering conspiracy of blind and heartless old men.

Yet despite everything, an astonishing volume of poetry survived, in the diaries the soldiers kept, in the barely censored letters that officers could send back to loved ones (the enlisted men were confined to preprinted postcards provided by the army). Some of the poems that got written, like those of Siegfried Sassoon and Wilfred Owen and Ivor Gurney, were luminous for all their darkness, glimmers of light in the overwhelming gloom. Most poems weren't. They were broken, wounded attempts to articulate the incomprehensible, remarkable for the effort but not for the product.

Yet almost all of them — poets and poems alike — shared a uniqueness. It was not so much of treatment or of focus, but of persistent determination to comprehend their condition by composing poems. The poets, therefore, shared a fundamental similarity of intention. They were young men trying to explain to themselves the continued presence of beauty and particularity within a world of violence that had submerged, in the brutal lunacy of trench warfare, all familiar physical and mental signifiers in a cocktail of cordite, flying fragments of near-molten metal, mud, and human gore.

I didn't recognize the degree to which the lyric poetry of my generation followed the Great War model until I read Vera Brittain's verse-filled autobiographical account of the Great War and its aftermath, *Testament of Youth*, and saw how many of the British officer class headed for extermination wrote poems along the way. If you were to die, and these men quickly realized that this was their likely fate, then you wanted to explain why, if only to your own benighted senses. Trying to find some way to reconcile the hell they'd found themselves in with the continued existence of natural and human beauty, kindness, and other generous human qualities was at least a project over which they had some hope of control. Everything else that once seemed certain and serene had literally turned into madness.

The Great War, therefore, created a compelling frame, and verse in English had not ventured far beyond it by 1970, save in the attempts to widen the field that are Ezra Pound's *Cantos*, William Carlos Williams's *Paterson*, and perhaps Charles Olson's *Maximus Poems*.

And yes, this legacy of reconciling incomprehensible violence inflicted on the sensible innocent remains the problem of poets working today, even though the world conditions that made English lyric verse what it has been since the Great War have not existed for any Westerners for more than fifty years. First, the military conflicts since 1945 in which North Americans and Western Euros have been engaged have not more than nominally involved the educated classes. Not even the Second World War, with its vast increases in civilian casualties, saw anything close to the same degree of violence directed at the young and the educated. Vietnam, the war that captured and to some extent created the social imagination of my generation, was a war to which America sent mostly black kids and white rednecks to do the dying. Yet the same larks appear above the blighted landscape in the poems of my generation as can be seen in the poems of the British war poets, except that the hell beneath the wings of today's poets consists of incitements to purchase goods, eat mediocre, pre-processed foods, and suck up other entertainments meant to atomize and then replace political democracy.

Thirty-five years ago, when I began my pursuit of Pound, Williams, Olson, and their poetic heirs as my teachers and working models, I had no more than a vague sense of where the roots of poetry lay. Fifteen years later, when I stopped publishing, I still had no clue. I believed in the sense of beauty that is lyric poetry's purest energy, but I was instinctively suspicious of the darkness that placed it in relief. What I perceived around me wasn't so much dark as muddy. It held no residue of high explosives, and it did not stream with human blood and body parts. It was fouled with cigarette butts and the paper and Styrofoam debris of mass-produced hamburgers and milkshakes. My instincts informed me that such a world requires a catalogue less private and idiosyncratic than Whitman's body electric, and an emotional frame less prone to self-regard and sentimentality than Wilfred Owen's pity. But I couldn't seem to create either catalogue or frame, and neither could my fellow poets.

At this point, I have a question of my own: Did the distinction I made in the 1980s between poetry and verse cause me to lose touch with an essential element of a writer's craft? I had a lot right in that 1980s essay. Like Edmund in Shakespeare's *King Lear*, I had seen the business, and like Edgar, I didn't like it. But poetry *is* an essential mode of human thought. It holds the technical protocols of metaphor, which is human language's most powerful but hardest-to-master instrument. Verse, on the other hand, is a temporary cultural expression of poetry, one that has been in a state of cognitive arrest for nearly eighty years. It is now pragmatically obsolete except as an underused training tool for writers working in still-viable genres, and its decay is a danger to the health of language because poetry's diminished purpose is not widely or accurately recognized by those who ought to recognize it. It simply aggravates the general offence that verse is sometimes given an official dignity and grandeur that poets — outside of those war poets — have had no way of earning.

Today it is hard for even the diehard partisans of verse to deny that the affective poetry of the late twentieth century lies in the products of popular culture created by commercial technologists, popular musicians, filmmakers, and videographers. Popular culture being what it is, the tools of poetry are now used to sell consumer commodities and intensify emotions, not to impart any sense of beauty or deliver crucial information. As an essential investigative tool and mode of thought, poetry is in a state of disuse, misuse, and disrepair that indirectly threatens the continued survival of the human species and, given all those nukes rusting in their missile silos, of life itself. Unfortunately, I don't have any practical suggestions about how to rectify this that won't require several years and two thousand pages to articulate.

Unbidden, or perhaps conditioned by my enhanced understanding of what twentieth-century lyric poetry was a response to, these new questions pop up: What about the therapeutic value of poetry? What's wrong with using poetry as a tool of self-exploration and an instrument of simple self-expression?

The poetry I wrote before I quit publishing was nearly always crudely self-expressive, and I moved on because my instincts told me that self-expression for a working writer is irrelevant. Then, perhaps ironically, I spent a decade teaching prison inmates cultural literacy in various disguises: creative and technical writing, history, and English literature courses. During those years I came to see how fundamental the urge to self-expression is in periods of crisis. Whether the crises are private, legal/criminal, or global doesn't seem to matter. Prison showed me how much more productive and pleasant life is for everyone when the urge to express oneself is trained and educated — however slightly we were able to accomplish that inside a jail. It made me change my mind about the uses of poetry as self-expression.

Perhaps the vast majority of written verse today ought to be viewed as self-expressive therapy and quietly treated not as art but as an important and effective kind of self-administered education that can bring order to the situationally confused or the chronically puzzled. If verse is to survive, perhaps this is where and how it should do so, as a minor but useful cultural instrument for ameliorating human stupidity and the violence that springs from it. At its best, verse therapy will refine some rough or confused minds. At the very least it will keep a few savage beasts from maiming the people around them. As we used to say in jail, reflection is good in and of itself, if only because it slows people down.

Yet in spite of everything I've said here about the state of poetry, I can't shake the notion that when I stopped publishing verse and thumbed my nose at the Biz, I gave up some access points to an essential life business. That being so, there are a couple of questions left that need answers: Is there anything genuine and valuable in the verse Biz? Are there substitutes for one who gives it up? Are there alternatives?

The short answers seem to be: (1) Yes. (2) Sure, but they don't work very efficiently, and for me they don't bring the same pleasures. (3) No, I can't think of any, but maybe others can. The longer answers go like this:

(1) I'll concede this much to the poetry Biz: It allows a few talented people to work with language at a complex level without constantly scrambling for subsistence or being bullied into obsessing over financial investments the way most of us are encouraged to do. I'm thinking not just about the few pissy grants the government doles out to working poets, but also about our university literature departments, which is where many poets end up, god help them. The benefits society receives from having such people around may seem out of measure with the fiscal costs incurred, but there's no reason that ought to bother us. The poet-professors are very small fish, whether they're the marginalized grant-accepting ones or the tenured academy ones. Their pond is small and drying up, and if we're serious about societal waste we'd do better to examine the armed forces, Parliament, or the health care system. If we think it's time to pry a few remora off society's fat haunches, that's where the big, slimy ones come from. We ought to praise these poets for what they are doing — removing bits of rust from the language we use. Or at least, that's what they're supposed to be doing.

(2) For good or bad, poets form communities. They do it for mutual support, whether the support involves editing, ego boosting, or simply companionship in their marginalized state. No other writers seem capable of doing this. It reveals something that the last fifty years of lyric poetry seemed determined to deny: That poetry is, at root, a social activity and that the choir, even if it is

only practising for imaginary or trivial recitations, is more important than the individual poet whining about his or her outcast fate. And unless we're addled enough to believe that singing in the shower makes us musicians and poets (which I don't), those of us who eschew the community aspect of poetry give up both a basic responsibility and a compositional comfort.

It therefore follows that it is incumbent upon poets to hang out, play the music, join the choir if they are to exercise their faculties. For good or bad, I haven't done that, and it bothers me. I've been asking myself lately whether I abandoned verse because I am, by nature, more solitary than the poets I grew up with. I am, but not because I'm less playful. I do note that my play preference is for matters of cognition, not music, and that my early life did leave me with a number of performance disabilities I've never much wanted to get over.

When I was younger, I played ball with my fellow poets (literally and figuratively), I slept with some of them, and I fought them over ideas and sometimes over lovers. At the time I thought those were essential pursuits of poetry and had nothing to do with being young. Today it is the conversation around poetry I miss more than I do the sex or the baseball or being young and confused. I've learned that poets carry friendships they form around language into old age, whereas nearly all other writers become more solitary and grumpily competitive. I miss that playful part of writing, and not just out of nostalgia. I miss the choir practices even though I never sang in tune with the choir. People who sing or play musical instruments keep their music nearby and in the open. People who work with ideas or characters in imagined landscapes keep them pinched, private, and where the sun don't shine nearly enough.

(3) Substitutes? I guess I could learn to be a nicer person and a more social one, and I could be more insistent about phoning my fiction/documentary writer friends and asking them about what they're working on — never mind that this makes them behave like threatened iguanas. Or I could admit that I'm really

a poet and see what that provokes. Now that I've tired of imposing myself on the world, maybe I can make something worthwhile from the larks flying overhead and from the guns and the bones and the hamburger wrappers. I could also go the opposite direction: answer all my e-mail, join a political party again, or take culture jammers and other activists more seriously. Or I could bite the big bullet and learn to play guitar, but didn't a guy named Leonard Cohen already do that en route to disappearing down a Zen rabbit hole? We'll see.

Finally, there's the question that this particular investigation begs to have me ask: Is writing — in any form that makes it a cognitive investigation of the universe (as opposed to an exploitation of a limited opportunity or market) — worth doing even when society doesn't recognize it as valuable? And if it is, what are the best ways to proceed in the twenty-first century?

I don't have the answers to those questions, and I won't pretend that I do. But I do understand better now than I did thirty years ago that poetry involves work, and that labour is both its greatest pleasure and its ultimate reward. Work is the one element of poetic composition that seemed to get lost in the trenches of the Great War — the poets merely hunkered down in the mud and waited to be killed. What I didn't understand adequately when I wrote the essay for Metcalf was that metaphor requires constructive practice more than it does rich human experience, which is about as useful and affective to it as second-hand cigarette smoke. So I'm tempted here to urge the notion that the essence of being human is the constructive practice of metaphor, and the expert exercise of it, particularly as it becomes a form of increasingly arcane behaviour, is crucial to our survival as an intelligent species.

But today I do so on something less than idealistic terms and projectives. Recent theories have it that it was a cognitive leap in Neolithic *Homo sapiens* which enabled our distant ancestors to see in metaphoric terms for the first time, that led them to exterminate the Neanderthal populations with whom they'd lived in relative peace for thousands of years. Metaphor, among its sanguine properties, offers the cognitive technologies for collective hysteria and the possibility of demonizing entire groups. That resonates through subsequent history in a sobering way. Metaphor itself may be the active agent in totalized wars and genocide. At very least it suggests that metaphor is a blade with two sharp edges. Then again, the only possible remedy to metaphor's misuse — whether it is by early *Homo sapiens* or Hitler or today's advertising technicians — is practice and work. Which I need to stop yapping about and get down to once again.

Versus Virus ⟩

IN THE SUMMER OF 2001, the Starbucks Corporation announced that it planned to open an outlet on Toronto's Bloor Street West, a block away from Dooney's Café where I write for a couple of hours most days. Shortly before the Starbucks opened, I got a call from a woman at CBC Radio asking me if I had any comment on the announcement. She was calling me because I had been among the dozen or so people who organized a successful fight against a 1995 attempt by Starbucks to close Dooney's and replace it with one of their outlets.

The 1995 event started with what appeared to be a done deal, but it soon transpired that the building landlord had sold the lease to Starbucks without offering a renewal to Dooney's Café proprietor Graziano Marchese, which made it unethical and subject to litigation. Graziano sued the landlord, but more important, the patrons of Dooney's quickly created a public relations nightmare for Starbucks, accusing the corporation of neighbourhood-busting and subjecting it to a series of embarrassing demonstrations organized by the media-savvy writers and others who've used Dooney's as a hangout for many years. They — we, I guess — organized the protests because we didn't want to lose the café and because we like Graziano and didn't want to have him replaced by an American franchise with minimum-wage *barristas*.

Those of us who are close to Graziano understood that the real villain in the piece wasn't Starbucks but the building landlord, an architect with a reputation for community-sensitive projects. As with most architects, designing and living were not the same thing for him. He recognized that having a corporate tenant with a long lease would vastly inflate the value of the building, which he would then turn over to some willing buyer — and "screw you" to both Graziano and the community.

After some early slithering, Starbucks did the right thing. It swallowed the lease, rented the premises to Graziano as a subtenant — and bought several full-page ads in the *Toronto Star*, making it clear that Starbucks wasn't in business to break up the neighbourhood and its institutions. The building landlord eventually lost the court case, which cost him some of the profits from selling the building. He left town, the stink dissipated, and life went back to normal on Bloor West.

I did have some comments to make about the opening of a Starbucks outlet on Bloor Street, but I quickly got the sense that my viewpoint on the story wasn't what the CBC woman wanted. She was looking for some doom-and-gloom sound clips, something to the effect that I was appalled, indignant, and incensed that Starbucks was opening nearby — or strained, worried, or terrified about what this would do to Dooney's. I wasn't appalled, and I wasn't frantic with worry, I told the woman, and I didn't think many others were, either. It's a free country, and Starbucks can do business wherever it likes. Then I went on to talk about the general effect of consumer franchises — for which I use the shorthand term "Virus" — filtering into the Bloor West streetscape, and about the fundamental differences between corporate and local culture.

The strip of Bloor Street West on which Dooney's sits has, like every other street in North America, been gradually delocalizing and corporatizing with Virus since the early 1980s. Taco Bell arrived in the early 1990s, along with a McDonald's down the street and a Pizza Pizza. Two years ago a Friendly Greek outlet opened, starved for customers for a couple of months, and then conveniently burned down and was closed permanently. A few months later a Tim Hortons opened up across the alley from it, and a Mr. Sub has now moved into the Friendly Greek location. In the blocks east of

Dooney's there is a series of second-tier food franchises, most of them serving the current food rage, sushi, and most are languishing. This is a mutable neighbourhood, with the only detectable trends being the likelihood of more Virus, and the gradual but apparently inexorable onslaught of Koreans, who now have the blocks west of Dooney's solidly locked up and are beginning to filter across Bathurst Street by opening up all-night cyber-café/convenience stores in which the operators survive by supplying the cheap labour themselves.

Dropping a Starbucks into this melange isn't, in other words, exactly a catastrophic event. And as Virus goes, Starbucks is far from the worst and will likely have a greater effect on the Tim Hortons at mid-block and the Second Cup franchise across the street from it than on Dooney's.

Having given a version of this thumbnail sketch of the street and the general conditions of its retail culture to the slightly impatient CBC woman, I tried to get her to understand that the important issue wasn't whether Starbucks is the spawn of Satan, but that the culture of Virus is gradually replacing local culture on Bloor West — and everywhere else. I could tell that this was all very interesting to her, but not a chaseable news item. If I wasn't going to be burning crosses in front of the new Starbucks, she needed to find someone who wanted to. I wished her luck and she hung up, her parting tone implying that I ought to be vaguely ashamed of myself for passing up the opportunity to be newsworthy.

I wasn't moved by her logic. Real life, along with its truly affective issues, frequently isn't newsworthy, or at least doesn't parse for the one-dimensional cliché-mongering that passes as daily news. Life, thankfully, is more grainy and less dramatic than news reporting, which is much more interested in smash-ups and broken legs than in complex ideas. Dooney's Café is one of those complex ideas. It works as a restaurant and as a local cultural institution almost solely because of Graziano Marchese, a short, dark, good-looking man in his mid forties who is anything but a walking cliché. Graziano is sweet-tempered and mercurial at the same time, absent-minded, slightly hard of hearing. He is also quick-witted and perceptive.

Despite his blue eyes, he's wholly Italian (Calabrese, as most of Toronto's 600,000 Italians are), but like most of the second-generation Italians, he's competently cosmopolitan. He's famously discreet if you need to sit and work, but if you want to talk about anything, he's up for it — if he's not on the phone trying to cajole a contractor to finish the renovations on his mother's house or fielding a catering order. He's a human being, in other words, as idiosyncratic and particular as Virus is *not*.

Dooney's has the same virtues. The quality of the food goes up and down depending on who's in the kitchen. Right now the dinner menu is well beyond merely good-and-serviceable thanks to chef Joe Tucci, and that has made the outdoor patio in full summer, surrounded by night-scented nicotiana, both a culinary and olfactory treat. A couple of years ago the lunch menu was the highlight, and at other times it has been weekend brunch or late-night desserts. The menus change with each chef, not because of corporate market research into what the largest number of people will buy at optimal profitability to head office, but because some cooks are better than others. No Dooney's menu gets subjected to a focus group. They get tested on Bloor Street's version of the real world. The only focus groups I've encountered at Dooney's are the impromptu kind, and when they don't quickly dissolve into silliness and laughter, their recommendations generally get ignored by Graziano, who pretends not to understand — or even hear — what they're trying to bully him into. "I just want to make people happy" is his standard reply. It means "Leave me alone, I've had enough."

The pleasure and value of Dooney's, and of local culture, lie in this sort of specificity. Where the attentions within local culture are weak or absent, it produces squalor — and most of the time that quickly leads to oblivion. When attentions are focused, as they usually are at Dooney's, they produce unique pleasures. Unique pleasures — and pains — tell us where we are. Dooney's, for instance, could only exist in Toronto, and more precisely, only in Toronto's west side, with its large Italian population that seems to respond best to the city's richly humid summers and its relaxed and often merry diversity. Dooney's clientele includes a contingent of mostly left-wing Italians, a loose mix of Anglo or Jewish academics, writers, visual artists, and people from the creative side of television and film. There is a group of elderly Hungarians who show up most afternoons, parking their handicapped-placarded cars higgledy-piggledy along Borden Street. There is also a sizable bunch of middle-aged women who aren't quite definable as either strictly lesbian or feminist, and seasonal convergences of students, tourists, and uptowners. It's very downtown Toronto, which means that the crowds are civil, tolerant, confident enough of their welcome that they don't feather up like tribesmen, occasionally noisy or demanding, fun to observe, and without a detectable single commercial denominator unless it involves, as filmmaker Michael Moore recently discovered in *Bowling for Columbine*, a penchant for leaving their front doors unlocked or open during the summer.

Virus operates differently. It creates comforts by hyperventilating a market denominator, one that is generally aimed both low and common, and always without any of the edges haphazard specificity brings. When you enter a franchise, you cease to be in any specific place other than a profit-generating nexus. When you go to Starbucks or Tim Hortons or McDonald's, you're there to consume their products and to be comforted by their artificial environment, which is designed to obliterate particularity. There's nothing wrong with this, by the way. A lot of people have miserable or disappointing or nerve-wracking lives, and the environment each Virus seeks to create provides respite from the sometimes unpleasant particularities that surround people in their daily lives.

It has been argued, sometimes eloquently by writers like Joshua Meyrowitz in his 1986 book *No Sense of Place*, and more often hysterically by populist sociologists and architects, that Virus is a powerful factor in what is depriving post-modern human societies of a sense of physical particularity and meaningful community. It is true that franchising consumer corporations — along with the whole set of economic tropes we're now characterizing as "globalization" — seek to denominate people into profitable and easily manipulated markets, and that they frankly don't give a shit about individuality or indigenous cultures. Why should a corporation want to foster those? Corporations are about profits and shareholders — and maybe, as we're now finding out, excessive and undeserved management bonuses and stock options. To ask corporations to respect the specific integrity of any local community is like asking a pig to fly.

That said, if the current economic *Zeitgeist* prevails, there's a point somewhere in the not-so-distant future when Bloor West will cease to be a specific, dynamic place and will become another unlocated strip mall. There are lots of those already, and they seem to be generating a new form of human hell. The ten-kilometre stretch of highway north of Kelowna, B.C., is the most spectacularly depressing one I can think of, but I'm subliminally able to recognize hundreds of others, and I'm reliably informed that such environments now number in the tens of thousands across the continent, each with kilometre after kilometre of Virus scrambling to entice consumers to low and common market denomination. They're each forms of hell, social consumption without society, civility, or community, comfort without location or individuation.

I don't want to live in or by or even near any of them. I was raised in a small town where I knew nearly everyone, and I grew up expecting that part of a normal life was having a fundamental understanding of what the people around me did and why they did it. That I ended up living in a downtown neighbourhood in Canada's largest city — the most culturally diverse city in the world — is no accident. Downtown Toronto's west side, along with a couple of other downtown neighbourhoods in Canada's major cities, are among the only functional small towns left in the country, and the only places we have where cultural specificity and civic particularity thrive. In its most simple formulation that means that I know my butcher, baker, grocer, and tailor by their first names, like I did forty years ago. It isn't heaven, but it does offer the basis for civil happiness, if such a thing exists outside a formula.

It happens that I've gotten to know Graziano Marchese better than any of the people who make up my neighbourhood, and my life is very much the better for it. I play baseball with him in the summer, I celebrate New Year's with him and his extended family, and during the late summer I take great pleasure in going with him to the wholesale farmers' market at the Ontario Food Terminals to buy tomatoes and peppers and wild blueberries and peaches and the other locally produced foods that the corporations can't match in quality or price because their profit manuals tell them it's easier and more profitable to truck such things in from California and Florida. Graziano, along with the daily fare at Dooney's, makes life sweet and specific, for me and for a lot of other people.

Meanwhile, Starbucks has come to Bloor West. Ho-hum. You won't catch me there, huddled around its market nexus, soaking up its artificial comforts with the estranged and the alienated.

The Purpose
of Paranoia

IN THE FALL OF 1997 I experienced an intellectual meltdown. It was caused partly by my having quit smoking at the beginning of the year, partly by physical exhaustion after the birth of my daughter in July, and partly because I was stopped dead on the book I'd been working on since 1990. But what lay beneath this was a cognitive spiral I'd been trapped in for several years, which I could neither resolve nor escape from. Since the 1970s there had been a world-wide slide away from social democracy and civility. A paradigm, which I'll get to in a moment, explained it, but I couldn't reconcile the paradigm with the data I'd accumulated, even though nearly all the data was corroborative. What I had on my hands was an encompassing but very chilly abstraction of what I could see occurring on the streets and in people's minds. Circumstantial stress and my native mental laziness made me want something more monstrous and villainous than an abstract paradigm — something dramatic enough to galvanize me, and others, to action.

The specific trigger for the meltdown came when the anti-consumerist magazine *Adbusters* asked me to write for them. I liked the general intentions of *Adbusters*, but I wondered how far I could go before running afoul of its faintly puritanical devotion to anti-consumerism. When that devotion occasionally reached a hysterical pitch, it amounted to bullying others into rejecting the things that, for better or worse, provide most of the fun in contemporary life.

I wrote — or tried to write — a piece for *Adbusters* explaining the paradigm and its effects. The result was the most incoherent piece of writing and thinking I've ever committed to paper. It was conceptually garbled, disjointed, filled with near-lunatic asides and leaps in logic, and it was even less grammatical than my usual early drafts. That wasn't traumatic in and of itself because, for me, writing is a string of necessary humiliations. Beyond that was something more disturbing: an underlying paranoia, evinced by paragraph-by-paragraph assurances that I wasn't nuts, that what I was trying to describe was out there, like the proverbial fox in the henhouse, but was too elusive to grasp. It was a new kind of paranoia for me, one that I couldn't seem to fit words around without having to resort to shouting. Even then . . .

I stopped working on the piece when I began to resort to a version of the "three kinds of people in the world" simplification that has tempted me in the past when I can't figure things out. This one proposed that there are a few people who attempt to live their lives in the service of basic notions of justice and human equality; other people — the vast majority of the world's population — who are too hungry or otherwise beaten down to care; and finally, amoral, opportunistic assholes.

It wasn't that this troika was any loonier than past ones I'd entertained, nor that I had — or have — serious misgivings about dividing up human beings this way, provided that the divisions are for laughs. This particular division was logical enough, in a reductive sort of way. What was wrong with it was that I was on the edge of applying it seriously. The assholes seemed to be everywhere I turned. They were aggressive and proud of their aggression, and they were shouting down every other voice, including my own. I was shouting back, but I wasn't making solid contact with anything beyond my initial simplification. They were assholes, alright, but rationally I knew most of them were neither monstrous nor evil and that my paranoia was convincing me they were. I put the piece in the drawer, ashamed of myself and frightened that I might be losing my stuff, and I didn't write again for nearly six months.

I've survived the meltdown, obviously. My daughter got beyond her infancy, my wife and I began to sleep at night, and eventually my life returned to the approximation of writerly concentration possible with a chattering toddler near its centre. I started dooneyscafe.com to help me get my chops back, and the stopped book even started to move forward, slowly, like an iceberg. But I remained frightened about what I'd written and my collapse in the face of its difficulty. The piece stayed in the drawer until I stumbled across it a few months ago. When I reread it I was astounded by its incoherence, the bad grammar and spelling, and the broken confidence and uncertainty it testified to. I knew I needed to fix it, or at least translate the intellectual debris into some semblance of English. I recovered the computer file, corrected the obvious spelling and grammatical errors, and printed it out.

From the original three thousand-word rant I've been able to recover only the two paragraphs that contained the paradigm. They aren't in their original form here, but they're close enough to be accurate representations. Here's what I had written:

The development and unimpeded ascendance of extra-national and trans-activity corporations as a political and social force that supplants local custom and culture, with the global marketplace as the sole generator of human polity, is the most important political development since the military defeat of Nazi Germany. This development constitutes a fundamental alteration of human activity, one that has met, thus far, virtually no effective political or cognitive opposition, and has generated an oligarchy of apparently unassailable influence and power.

The Bosnian dramatist Dzevad Karahasan, in a 1993 book titled Sarajevo, Exodus of a City, *argues that it was a new civil paradigm and not traditional ethnic hatreds that destroyed his city and country: "economic and technical openness coupled with semantic and cultural closure." He describes a societal condition where commodity trade, currency, and technical innovation flow through unimpeded, the right to financial profit subsumes all other rights, while the crucial discourse over the meaning of words withers and people cease to be able to communicate across their differences. This, and not a hodgepodge of festering ethnic and religious grievances, he argues, was what transformed the city of Sarajevo from the jewel of non-imperialist socialist democracy into a rubble-littered zone of unreasoning hatred, human slaughter, and environmental destruction.*

I didn't believe that this paradigm explained every event across the former Yugoslavia, or the intensity and senselessness of the violence. That requires a different, and more specific, analytic nexus, one that includes local motives, personality, and opportunity. But I was convinced that this paradigm played a powerful role, and that it has also invaded institutions and customs in every other nation and geography across the planet over the past twenty-five years. It applies to every society, without exclusion. The relative absence of violence in Western Europe and North America so far — even after September 11, 2001 — suggests that our short-term outcomes will be different from those in the former Yugoslavia. Still, our political and cultural institutions are no less undermined. Western democracies are now thoroughly restrained by the trade agreements they've signed, which have given corporate entrepreneurs freedoms from the restraints of national and local government statutes and regulations not offered to individual citizens. What Karahasan's paradigm describes are the core processes of what we now understand as "globalization," a revolution on behalf of the rich, or, more accurately, the rights of money and capital to accumulate and be moved without interference.

Globalization is normally depicted as an unspecified set of inevitable economic evolutions brought on by advances in technology and communications. It is generally conceded that there are cultural and even political consequences, but that these are of little concern to those who have exploited the evolutions to create multinational trade and financial apparatuses. Globalization, inevitable or not, is now a "fact of life" for every society on the planet. But "globalism," the philosophical base by which globalizing processes are justified, has no locatably stable existence, physically or conceptually. It exists as a shadowy threat in the minds of those who oppose the forces and the specific manifestations of globalization, and it clearly exists as the nebulous elan of multinational corporations and of many of the people who work for them.

The roots of globalism are lodged in the First World War, where the incompetence of the political duelling between Europe's nation-states resulted in the largely pointless deaths of almost 10 million young men. The defeat of Nazi-Fascism in the Second World War, which seemed to validate constitutional democracy and laid a slight stigma upon cooperation between corporations and governments, delayed its advance almost a quarter century.

Thus its contemporary roots lie in the 1973 energy crisis brought on by the formation of the OPEC cartel and, secondarily, in the debacle of the Vietnam War. But the seeds were planted in the 1960s and nourished by the unrest and riots that swept across Europe and North America in 1968 — and by the apparent inability of Western governments to maintain the status quo and, more important, to stem the downward redistribution of wealth and privileges that had been occurring since the First World War and was accelerated by the Second World War. By the late 1970s, corporate heads were stepping out of their boardrooms and onto the soapboxes, employing their massive communications resources to lobby openly for capitalist values and — not incidentally — to transform corporate captains into de facto cultural leaders. Lee Iacocca was the first of these, but thousands have followed. Within a few years they quietly captured the *Zeitgeist* and have since successfully reversed the distribution of wealth that had been flowing downward — as a conscious political principle — since 1918. Now, two decades after Iacocca stepped into the limelight, we have a world conspicuously and openly defined, politically and culturally, by capitalist economic practices.

A description by the American philosopher Richard Rorty is worth offering here in its somewhat rhetorical completeness:

The central fact of globalization is that the economic situation of the citizens of a nation state has passed beyond the control of the laws of that state. It used to be the case that a nation's laws could control, to an important and socially useful extent, the movement of that nation's money. But now that the financing of busi-

ness enterprise is a matter of drawing upon a global pool of capital, so that enter-
prises in Belo Horizonte or in Chicago are financed by money held in the Cay-
man Islands by Serbian warlords, Hong Kong gangsters and the kleptocrat presi-
dents of African republics, there is no way in which the laws of Brazil or the U.S.
can dictate that money earned in the country will be spent in the country.

We now have a global overclass which makes all the major economic deci-
sions, and makes them in entire independence of the legislatures, and a fortiori
of the will of the voters, of any given country. The money accumulated by this
overclass is as easily used for illegal purposes, such as supplying land mines to
the latest entrepreneurial warlord or financing gangster takeovers of trade
unions, as it is for legal ones. The absence of a global polity means that the
super-rich can operate without any thought of any interests save their own.
(Richard Rorty, "Globalization and the Politics of Identity" in
Philosophy and Social Hope [London: Penguin, 1999], p. 233)

Rorty is mistaken in one part of this. We *do* have a global polity
because the forces of globalization force us to relate to the world
through the terms and conditions of a global marketplace, whether
we want to or not. Socially and culturally we've already descended
into an approximation of George Orwell's *Animal Farm*: All animals
are equal, but some are more equal than others. The operators of
corporations can move capital and personnel much more easily than
individuals or local capitalists can. And because the on-site pigs
aren't really running the farm, every minority has been set against
the others as each tries not to land on the wrong side of the new
scales of equality. With the preferred model of polity that of competition, individuals and groups are competing culturally — not for
monetary wealth, but for the values that globalization has no way of
manufacturing or controlling: dignity and authentication. This competition is the unacknowledged element of globalization, and com-
pletes it as a system of human relations. The only thing missing is
the formal write-up.

No one saw this coming. Twenty-five years ago I believed, along
with most American liberals and social democrats elsewhere in the
West, that those responsible for undermining democracy and

human cognitive stability were likely to be some combination of the U.S. government and the military-industrial complex, the latter of which was the shorthand Dwight D. Eisenhower used to warn his successors about the gaggle of wastrel weapons-development-and-supply corporations guarded by an oligarchy of intelligence spooks, war-hawk generals, corporate plutocrats, and appointed government operatives. Despite Eisenhower's warning, the military-industrial complex owned the presidency of Richard Nixon and was actually if not officially responsible for the illegal and unconstitutional extension of the Vietnam War into neutral Cambodia, which eventually saw a half million tons of explosives dropped and roughly 750,000 civilians dead. The complex had the ordnance and wanted to expend it while developing even more effective weapons. This same configuration, during the Reagan administration, went on to spend the USSR into oblivion with the Star Wars defence initiative, and since the Eisenhower era it has carried on innumerable illegal and clandestine operations in Central and South America, and — usually less effectively — in other parts of the "impoverished" world. It was, in other words, ugly and comfortingly monstrous.

The military-industrial complex was sometimes spectacularly successful in achieving its narrow goals, which were to make the United States the sole military superpower in the world and to make the weapons-producing corporations filthy rich in the process. But it was also tremendously expensive and prone to overkill, figuratively as well as literally. It and its owner-operators had a penchant for working in the shadows, which made it difficult for its captains to exert power openly, and made the complex assailable by the liberal leftists who believed that the public realm should be the seat of effective power.

Subsequent revelations about the conduct of the Vietnam War, and the release of the Pentagon's training manuals for Central and Latin America, shed an eerily clear light on just how far into the politically and morally opaque the owner-operators of the military-industrial complex were going to win the Cold War and impose their worldview on "undeveloped" countries. The U.S. military created the School of the Americas to train sixty thousand officers from various Latin American military affiliates to do pretty much what the most strident leftist conspiracy weirdos claimed they were doing: torturing, mutilating, or disappearing anyone who opposed them. The daily reality in those countries, we now know, was on the far edge of the worst nightmares of the liberal/left weirdos.

Finding out that the weirdos weren't cracked is an unsatisfying sort of comfort, as it must have likewise been for the right-wing weirdos when it became evident that every horror they'd ascribed to Stalin and the Soviet Union was accurately depicted, and then some. The thrill of being right has little value when you remember that after-the-fact knowledge provides no comfort to the victims and does little to better the lives of those still living in those countries. But it does raise some interesting questions about conspiracies and common sense, and about how nasty and manipulative people with a nose for power will become to get it. Unfortunately, it also creates a kind of autonomic hypervigilance that misleads.

The military-industrial complex, for instance, continues to exist in the twenty-first century. The Clinton administration forced it into a slightly truncated and more international form by curbing U.S. military spending and putting a leash on the more violent kinds of clandestine intelligence operations. Even so, the armaments corporations spent the 1990s filling small countries like Bosnia with land mines, just as they had done in Southeast Asia in the previous decades, but the new mines are harder to detect and might be manufactured anywhere, under licence. During the 1990s, the military-industrial complex spent its energies maintaining international business contacts or enhancing the competence of its sales force at global arms bazaars in various Third World portals of violence, content to operate this way until George W. Bush took the U.S. presidency, brought a horde of Cold War spooks out of the shadows, and mixed them with the Christian fundamentalists who have long been yammering at the edges of the Republican party. The Bush administration sometimes seems intent on starting the twenty-first-century crusades. In those shadows, the military-industrial complex is making a comeback, this time as the dutiful police department of globalism. It is less stridently militaristic now, less controlled by governments, and much more corporate in character. It has contributed enthusiastically to demonizing national governments, along with their vague ideas about social and political justice. But it isn't seen as running the world anymore.

In the twenty-first century, what dictates government policy and shapes public opinion is much larger and harder to conceptualize than the military-industrial complex ever was. The captains of the New World Order, as it is sometimes called, are a convergence of the international banking system (led by the International Monetary Fund and the World Bank), the corporate commercial sector, and the corporate mass media into a technological and ideological juggernaut. This juggernaut has the power, influence, and slickness to make the old military-industrial complex seem bumbling and Neanderthal. Yet it does not, in the strict sense, have a corporeal existence and is easier to identify by its processes than by any coherently codified set of goals and objectives. Globalization is a reality, and "globalism" — at least in this assertion — is its value system and code book. It is proceeding with the reconstruction of human polity — and to some extent human reality — virtually unopposed except for a few thousand twenty-something North Americans and Western Europeans and their wooly-sweater-and-Birkenstock-wearing elders, many of whom look and act like Noam Chomsky, which is to say they're similarly humourless and too intent on rediscovering the military-industrial complex they'd become skilled at transfixing with impeccable moral logic.

Nearly all opposition to globalism is mired in a fundamental error in perception. It doesn't appear to recognize that the effects of globalization rarely identify the perpetrators. In some instances this is the error of social democrats, who characteristically believe governments ought to be in charge, even when they're evidently powerless. The opposers therefore assume — in practice if not in theory — that governments *are* the lead actors of globalization when there is convincing evidence that they're merely following orders. That's why the major anti-globalism demonstrations have been at G8 dumb-shows of heads of state or senior foreign or trade ministers instead of at the headquarters of the banks and the mega-corporations. The anti-globalists need to make corporations the target of their protests, and they also need to sharpen definitions of the globalist ideas that are responsible.

Globalism has successfully convinced nearly everyone, including those trying to oppose it, that democracy can continue only as barely regulated capitalism (and then only if people work from sunrise to sunset); that the layer of scum atop the bay outside our windows is the price we pay for competing in the global marketplace; and that those pale, chemical-infused egg yolks at the supermarket actually constitute a kind of efficiency that is sustainable and more beautiful and desirable than truth, beauty, or social justice. Those are all assailable notions that aren't adequately registered as the products of globalism, or are assailed primarily by pointing to the moral superiority and beauty of social democracy.

This constitutes a shift in consciousness and illustrates why globalism is the most effective and best-equipped-to-communicate oligarchy in human history. It has been powerful and pervasive enough that in little more than twenty years it has successfully imposed its cognitive DNA and vocabulary across every discursive and cultural frame for human interaction. As a result, Western societies are devolving from imperfect but functioning civil democracies into a vast matrix of competitive socioeconomic enclaves, between which the only identifiable commonality is their impulse to compete for whatever resource is at issue: rights, money, pleasure, righteousness, power, control of resources and people, and language itself. Globalism needs to be recognized as primarily an open cognitive and cultural program, and not depicted as a conventional political or economic conspiracy operated in an atmosphere of secrecy. It is also important to recognize that globalism is not aware of itself as an oligarchy, nor are its active players particularly aware of one another as collaborators. They simply believe, laconically and vocally, that economic values — primarily those of laissez-faire capitalism — ought to dictate the terms for other components in human life-support systems, that governments are incapable of economically sound behaviours, and that the less government we have the better.

In practice, and in its rudimentary theoretical formulations, globalism is a collection of short-focus business and capital transfer mechanisms, not a discrete entity or coherent system of values. That's less a comfort than it might seem, because it means that whatever mechanism is in play has an organizing logic and a direct purpose but is without any self-awareness of an overreaching mission. It therefore has no instinct — or capacity — to seek balance between its components and does not respond to internal contradictions as an organic system will. Like all mechanical systems, it conducts its activities without foresight, hindsight, or compassion. If queried or confronted, its claim to legitimacy is pragmatic. In action, it can only pursue tangible, short-term goals without any context except that of the uncodified and completely simple-minded *sub rosa* entrepreneurial ideology that valorizes self-aggrandizement, selfishness, greed, and, sometimes, a willingness to employ political, cultural, or military violence to attain ends.

The oil crisis in 1973 and the U.S. military defeat in Southeast Asia renewed the conscious movement toward extra-national government because these two events made two truths incontrovertible to the classes that hold wealth and political power: (1) Planetary resources are finite and likely to become progressively more scarce, and (2) Conventional democratic political processes are not going to maintain profit levels or the socioeconomic status quo so long as they insist on continuing to redistribute wealth downward. OPEC was a kind of walking proof to the wealthy that their wealth now had to operate within a worldwide context, and that strangely dressed foreigners had to be included in their calculations and even in their social circles. The vulnerability of the military-industrial complex to military defeat by technologically inferior forces was publicly interpreted as a result of liberal democratic excesses — fellow travellers — not as an outcome of technological excesses or poor sociopolitical strategies. But a more important message got through to the wealthy: Militarists are too obsessed with firing weapons to be trusted with the money and power.

Globalism's improved efficiency over previous systems of human control is tied to the swiftness and skill with which it morphs to meet hindrances to its short-term goals. The formative — and still controlling — evolution appeared after a worldwide bout of inflation in the early 1980s, when runaway inflation seriously eroded the holdings of wealthy classes, which, to that point, probably didn't recognize that their interests might be different from those of the military-industrial complex or the productive elements of the economy. What ensued was a fundamental redesign in Western monetary systems aimed at keeping inflation at artificially low levels to protect accumulated wealth and capital. The decade of occasionally feckless "deregulation" that followed was actually an attempt to achieve tax cuts and create a substantial widening of the real interest rate (prime lending rate minus inflation rate). That widening has been used to impoverish governments and citizens alike by making government and individual borrowing expensive. The government deficits that resulted, and the subsequent borrowing during the 1980s gave lenders an unprecedented degree of control over governments and made possible what all Western countries experienced in the 1990s: the curtailing of government budgets, services, and the social entitlements of individual citizens. Governments are now supplicants of the bond marketers and their rating agencies, the transfer of assets from the public to the private sector continues, and monetary and trade policy have become the dominant if hard-to-perceive cultural discourse.

Not all of this has gone smoothly. The emergence of an unregulated and entrepreneurial management sector willing to commit fiscal piracy against its own shareholders points to the mechanical and binary elements of globalism. Because they're unguided mechanisms, they run until they break down or crash. There's no one even trying to guide globalism's cultural and political mechanisms beyond the moment of profit-taking, and that's a problem because culture and politics are human and dynamic systems that demand feedback if they are not to run amok. Under globalism, they are expected to trail docilely in the wake of the economic mechanisms. If something provides profits, it's okay. You see? There's the cognitive spiral that got me in 1997, and it is still active. And lurking with it, the paranoia.

William S. Burroughs, the patron saint of the generation that came of age in the 1960s, once joked that paranoia was the product of being in the vicinity of too many facts. He was right, but what he failed to add was that this is nothing new, and that it isn't so much a joke as a comment on a fundamental change in the human condition. What he had no way of knowing was that by the time the twenty-first century arrived, paranoia and too many facts would become defining elements of the human condition.

Now, I believe, as Primo Levi did, that the philosophical polarities human beings have always lived between (whether they recognize it or not) are the indeterminacy of the physical universe and unjustified human suffering, or as Levi had it, black holes and the story of Job. I also believe, again with Levi, that the active part of the human condition, the one we can do something about, is the task of constructing social and individual meaning between those two unpromising but realistic polarities.

Those of us who were educated in the first three decades after the Second World War were taught, from elementary school on, that human societies are or ought to be based on Kant's Categorical Imperative: "Act only on that maxim by which you can at the same time will that it should become a universal law" or, in the vernacular, "Don't screw other people if you aren't prepared to be screwed in the same way." At the root of this was a faith that enlightened self-interest did, or eventually — soon — would, govern essential individual and collective interactions.

But if we believed in the Categorical Imperative, we weren't nearly so sure that authority was benevolent, or that it could be. Nazi Germany and the Soviet Union had demonstrated what happened when authority was released from constitutional constraints and the rule of law, and that people with power would lie, manipulate, and commit acts of violence against citizens to maintain or enlarge their private interests. In that sense we were American cosmopolitans, which is to say spiritual heirs of Thomas Jefferson, who drafted the U.S. constitution with a near-pathological mistrust of authority and power.

This heritage should have helped my generation to see through globalism as soon as it appeared. It didn't, and I'm not sure why. Maybe it was because we believed in the Categorical Imperative as if *it* were the Apocalypse and thus in no further need of vigilance or defence. The barbarians were in permanent retreat from its self-evident truth. Maybe it was the drugs my generation took in the 1960s, which, while they opened and sharpened our physical senses, also made us self-indulgent and inward-looking. The events of 1968, thrilling as they seemed at the time, may also have convinced us that humane social democracy and non-denominational meritocracy were inevitable, the only course of evolution open beyond planetary self-immolation. I still believe the last of these is true, but now I understand that positive evolution isn't inevitable or even particularly common.

Whatever the cause, libertarians and social democrats alike conflated their mistrust of authority with government alone. It made the social democrats among us blind to the hijacking of government by extra-national corporations, and those of us on the libertarian side of the spectrum willing participants in the virtual overthrow of democracy to achieve economic stability and the unreasonably high levels of entrepreneurial self-determination and profit-taking that have replaced the Categorical Imperative as the core value of our polity. The result is that we're now serving the barbarians breakfast in our own kitchens every morning. They come in with the newspapers, over the radio and television. There are mornings when I'm no longer sure, in the maelstrom of facts, that I'm not one of them.

That's why I now see paranoia a little differently. It isn't merely a debilitating cognitive undertow that perpetually threatens to suck me into chaos. It has become an effective, if damaging, antibiotic against the disinformational overload that exhausts me and thus invites me to simplify or ideologize — or simply ignore — the world as it is.

How we see ourselves ought to be accompanied by doses of structural skepticism when everything else lies beneath a blanket of informational fog. Someone, or something, prefers us with our heads in our navels. Periodic attacks of paranoia signal that I'm probably seeing things as they are and that the meanings I construct and live by shouldn't be blinders to keep me on the straight and narrow to oblivion. Paranoia isn't pleasant to live with, but I'm beginning to think of it as the most reliable navigational instrument I have.

Chaos Theory and
Traffic Control

THE CITY I LIVE IN, TORONTO, is experiencing severe problems these days. They aren't caused by poor leadership, even though our current mayor, Mel Lastman, spends most of his energy cramming his foot into his mouth, and the mayor before him, a left-leaning woman named Barbara Hall, had the political delivery of a daycare supervisor, along with a similar intellectual range. Instead, they are the result of senior governments solving their ideologically inflicted budget problems by "downloading" capital and service costs to junior governments. As the biggest city in Canada, Toronto has taken a heavier download than any other, even in relative terms.

Toronto was recently identified by the United Nations as the world's most culturally diverse city, with Italian and Chinese populations over half a million, and enclaves of Poles, Portuguese, Caribbeans, Koreans, Somalis, and several South Asia ethnicities in excess of 100,000. There are violent criminal gangs within some of these enclaves, and the predictable shouting about racism. But it is accurate to call Toronto the safest and most culturally tolerant big city in North America and probably the world.

The pleasures of cultural diversity are well advertised: good food and music, a sometimes cosmopolitan elan, and a wider range of civilized and civilizing abilities present. When cities are as peaceful and safe as Toronto nearly always is, these qualities blossom. But they're not without their problems, particularly when it comes to providing immigrant services like ESL training, civil education, and medical screening. With the downloading of costs that has gone on over the last decades, budget day at City Hall tends to be characterized by loud weeping and wailing, along with the cleanup after the departmental knife-fights in the back corridors. Established citizens, who keep demanding a safer if not necessarily aesthetically enhanced urban environment by splattering slow-cooked Not-In-My-Back-Yard politics across every initiative, have helped make budgets even tighter.

In my particular downtown neighbourhood near College and Bathurst streets, this reached a strange sort of asinine apogee a couple of years ago. A mob of bicycle-using Anglo spiritual vegans hijacked the most influential ratepayer group and got the city's mysteriously flush Traffic Control Division to install "traffic calming" apparatuses throughout the streetscape. The ostensible purpose of the traffic calming was to put a stop to the antics of a dozen or so teenage jackasses who use the long north-south streets as speed tracks for their customized Honda Civics — thus jeopardizing a few slow-moving pedestrians and impinging on the bicylists' god-given right to cycle the wrong direction on the mostly one-way streets while meditating on the contents of their navels.

Contractors hired by the Traffic Control Division were soon installing speed control mounds every hundred metres along the streets, along with a ghastly-looking maze of concrete and brick impediments that causes traffic to swerve from one side of the road to the other and, theoretically, slow down. These impediments (the engineers have a suave-sounding technical term for them that I refuse to let cross my lips) also reduced street-parking capacities by between 20 and 30 percent, which quickly became a sore point with the Italians who make up about half the neighbourhood population. The bicyclists behind the "calming" plan had gotten it through by, among other things, telling everyone that there would be no reduction in street parking. When I asked one of the leaders about this, he told me they'd lied about it because, well, the benefits outweigh the inconveniences, and anyway, aren't we trying to get cars off city streets? They knew better, in other words, so lying was okay.

Among the many things I like about Toronto's Italians is that they take a dim view of being lied to. This, and the fact that they damned well wanted their parking back, moved them to petition the City to rethink the entire program. After a series of acrimonious confrontations at public meetings, the Traffic Control Division sourly agreed to remove *some* of the impediments, but only if they could increase the frequency of the mounds, and only then if everyone voted to confirm that this was what we wanted done. The Italians and Portuguese, willing to make the best of the poor alternatives they'd been offered, voted to remove. Even then the Traffic Control Division dragged its heels, removing the impediments — by now obscured by weeds and street debris — only after a fire truck found itself trapped in one of the mazes on Euclid Avenue by some illegally parked vehicles of College Street restaurant patrons. Curiously, the Division left behind several of the mazes, including the one that trapped the fire truck.

Other flaws in the general attempt to calm the traffic, meanwhile, have become apparent to anyone willing to spend ten minutes observing. The dozen kids in their Hondas are treating their former speed track as a rally course, decreasing their overall speed only slightly, if at all. While they're having more fun than ever, less-attentive and -skilled drivers generate a new hazard by not noticing the speed mounds until too late and losing control as they cross. "Normal" drivers quickly learned that the speed mounds are sloped at the edges in order to permit water to pass along the curb gutters, and they now regularly zip within inches of the sidewalks, splashing unwary pedestrians, threatening infants in their baby carriages, and creating a brand-new strain of maternal hysteria.

Exacerbating all this, the professionals at Traffic Control Division and their contractors installed the mounds with their predictable inattention to detail. Some mounds were higher than others, thus lulling test-the-limit drivers at one and punishing them at the next. This effect was heightened by the physics of roadway construction and vehicle weights, the results of which were depressions in front of and after many of the mounds. After a year or so of use, this raised the launch trajectories in alarming ways.

As an ex-urban planner, none of this idiocy surprises me. One of the reasons I left the field was my discovery that nearly all planners fall into one of two categories: those who are mis-trained and stupid, or those who are excessively convinced of the moral rightness of their woeful expertise. In my experience, traffic control engineers tend to suffer from both of these disabilities. They have been trained to hate private motor vehicles and to obstruct their use in whatever ways they can — unless they're building freeways for them, in which case they'll steal food from nursing mothers to aid construction. They operate on the theory that if they can make life miserable for private vehicle users, the users will stop using automobiles close to their homes and will stop parking them on the city streets. The theory, which is really a moral principle, remains, well, theoretical after forty years of application, possibly because for citizens who aren't obsessively anal and physically fit, there are no practical alternatives to the use of private motor vehicles short of unemployment and destitution.

Toronto's Traffic Control Division doesn't seem to give a damn about practical reality, nor do its engineers and flacks appear to understand that immigrant populations occasionally notice that the facilities provided in their neighbourhoods don't bear much resemblance to those installed for the comfort of wealthy Anglos living in the ritzier parts of town. The Euclid Avenue speed mounds, for instance, are barely a metre wide and are constructed of asphalt with white arrows painted (very temporarily) on them. They're ugly as well as poorly engineered. The ritzy speed mounds are lower, at least three metres wide, edged and bricked with ceramic or terra cotta tiles, and often incorporate elegant planters, which the city's workers regularly fill with flowers.

All these minor transgressions of democratic equality and common sense might be forgiven if the traffic calming devices actually calmed the traffic. But they don't, because the engineers are as ignorant of the inevitable effects of chaos theory as they are devoid of common sense or respect for democracy.

Chaos theory — as it pertains to traffic control — boils down to this: Any increase in the complexity of a system exponentially increases the likelihood that it will screw up. The more complicated you make something, in other words, the more likely it is to do the opposite of what you want it to. Instead of a streetscape in which a few kids occasionally drive too fast, we now have one in which those same drivers are swerving and braking while they drive too fast, and every other driver is swerving and braking at slightly lower speeds. The number of near-misses of pedestrians has increased tenfold, and now the danger is not merely to jaywalking pedestrians and wrong-way bicyclists, but to a much larger group that has to dodge the out-of-control vehicles that spend about as much time on the sidewalks as on the roadways.

The traffic calming devices continue to obstruct large emergency vehicles and have inflicted serious mechanical damage to the running gear of any number of cars and trucks. They have also made street sweeping and snow removal an ongoing nightmare — when it is done at all. One slightly paranoid theory I've heard is that the street-cleaning budget was given to the traffic calming nitwits. In total, traffic calming has not only failed to calm the traffic, it has also made the streets of the neighbourhood less safe and much dirtier — as any half-baked physicist could have predicted.

All of this leads up to a piece of advice I'd like to deliver to the elected representatives of budget-poor municipalities, whether they're in the City of Toronto or the tiniest municipality in the Northwest Territories. Here it is: If you want to enhance the quality of life for your citizens, make your streets safer, and reduce your budgetary shortfall so you can spend what little you have on programs that actually help people. I know how to do it. You should disband all the programs — and traffic calming isn't the only one — that propose life can be made safer by choking, hamstringing, or super-regulating people and the simply-evolved systems by which they interact and/or go about their daily business. In this particular instance it would involve reducing the traffic calming divisions to the meterpersons who write those revenue-enhancing parking tickets outside Starbucks and Tim Hortons. But on a larger scale it would reduce officiousness in government, give the auditor general a break, lower the level of irritation amongst the citizenry, and narrow, if ever so slightly, the gulf between the physics of bureaucracy (usually indistinguishable from human stupidity) and the physics of the rest of the universe.

Exile

IF I WERE TO MAKE A MOVIE about the last half of the twentieth century, it would be called *Exile*. Even though I have a pathological dislike of being photographed or filmed, I'd be onscreen in the film because I'd be obliged to narrate it. That requirement is enforced by the collapse of other means of testifying to what one understands that don't mask the distortion of information by its delivery technology. I would stand before my movie's camera with a discomfort that isn't simply personal. My presence there signals the completion of the cultural and cognitive shift from ground to figure that began to accelerate out of measure when René Descartes tried to prove the existence of God by using his senses and discovered that he could prove only that he was making the attempt in good faith. The more or less total completion of this shift has been the most damaging and least recognized accomplishment of the twentieth century. To be philosophically and technologically central but without ground is to be suspended above an abyss. Within its darkness lies not that which is unknown, but the disintegration of knowledge itself.

Curiously, this shift has contributed to making the governing conditions of daily life in the twenty-first century more commercial and technological than private, biophysical, or political. Now that life is wholly about the individual, the individual has become subservient to its appetites. If individual physical perception is the only credible means of judging reality, it is also the most vulnerable to manipulation, and the industrial apparatus invented to do this work over the last hundred years is immense and frequently overpowering.

It's clear to me that I have little control over the environments within which I exercise my faculties. The affective forces that shape the lives and the minds of those of us who live in the West today are corporate. They are usually remote, often administered from beyond national boundaries and local culture and customs, and nearly always outside of individual tactile reach. Most corporations are not now subject to the same laws and obligations as the citizens they affect, and only the most privileged and powerful individuals are able to alter their velocity and direction — if they can at all. Corporations have become a virtual life form, able to follow their own limited rules in pursuit of non-human and non-biological goals.

In the West, ubiquitous government and corporate advertorials claim that we live in a state of participatory democracy. The most fabulous lie of the Global Village is that being forced to live on sugar and then being given a choice about which sugar manufacturer to buy it from is a meaningful exercise in democracy. Thus my corollary judgment is that the democracy offered today is a specious conflation of individual human rights and civil responsibilities with commercial participation. Europeans and North Americans have abandoned their civil will — along with control over their appetites — to the corporations and to the cornucopia of products at the mall, choosing meaning through the distorting lens of manipulated consumer and cultural self-determination. We now are encouraged to pursue social justice only where it redresses the ethnic, racial, sexual, and gender-based grievances of our ancestors or our chosen co-partisans. Beyond that, we acquire and we consume commodities, and where we discriminate it is mainly between superior and inferior products. Our consumer habits dictate our private and public identities. Our politics are stunted and self-interested. Almost no one believes that the world will get better than it is right now, and we forget that improving the general quality of life is the true basis for democratic politics. The anti-globalist left has adopted the slogan

"An other world is possible." As one wag added, with rueful cynicism, "but not likely."

Other things also depress our politics. Most of us recognize that on the planetary scale, six billion people can't go to the mall. There just isn't enough product to go around, and not enough resources to let the majority live as we do. Westerners thus agree, simply by getting up in the morning, to the permanent poverty of other human beings. Further, the consumer choices we're offered boil down to a single choice between personal gratification and long-term biological life on the planet. Even this is a temporary choice, and, because it is possible only by the expenditure of resources that can't be renewed, ultimately terminal. That makes the aftertaste of the twentieth century redolent of sour ironies piled atop poisonous ones: Information technologies that destroy individual knowledge; grand experiments in human liberation that result in global injustices, deprivation, and social psychosis; commodity wealth that dooms our social environments to become armed security camps, and the natural world to decline or monoculture.

Among the sourest of those ironies, obscured by the globality of the others, is a seemingly minor one. The twentieth century's productive achievements can't be accurately calculated without considering their capacity for displacing and dispossessing the human beings whose lives they set out to liberate and enrich. Refugees and exiles are the dark side of self-determination because now that we are shoulder to shoulder in our vast numbers, we can't lay claim to paradise without taking it from someone else. Whether what we desire is national or ethnic or consumer self-determination doesn't matter. The pursuit of any of these reduces other people and things to ideological simplifications that enable exploitation and righteous violence, whether the target is entire populations or individuals trying to improve the conditions under which they live.

I've been lucky enough to have lived a materially privileged life in a privileged part of the world, but I have lived my lucky life in a state of exile that has multiple levels and aspects. It is the cognitive conditions of this state of exile that at once elicit my diffidence towards unrestricted self-determination and make me wary of self-expression. Both alienate me from common sense, commonwealth, and the future. Those cognitive conditions also make personal testimony the only authentic point of view from which, as a writer, I can examine and testify to the portion of the human condition about which I have exact knowledge. I don't like it, but this is the way things are.

The condition of cognitive and experiential exile mixed with relative physical and political security is peculiar to the economically privileged nations and classes, and it should be distinguished from conditions outside the "developed" societies and their economies, despite some structural similarities. The key factors are that, in relative terms, we're not starving, most of us have a roof over our heads when we want one, and our lives are rarely threatened by common and casual violence the way people's lives are in the rest of the world.

I don't feel as if I'm anybody's or anything's victim. But I recognize that the comparatively safe and secure conditions under which I live share several of the most demoralizing characteristics of life in less wealthy and stable societies: Cultural disorientation and alienation; the inability to recognize and protect mutually supportive social, political, and economic interests; the inability to establish and pursue long-term goals beyond the millisecond of gratification or near-term expedience. Each of these exiles me from social solidarity and sometimes from meaning itself.

Not sure of this? Try seeing self-determination, as it is pursued under post-Cold War capitalism, in terms of what it *doesn't* permit, and what it disables. For instance, only a small minority of those of us who live in the "developed world" now get to live our lives in a contiguous landscape or civil stage. Only a tiny fraction of this minority can say that their human and physical habitations bear any resemblance to the ones they were born into. Fewer still experience life as a continuity and a coherence or have a sense of community that does anything other than seek to defend an arbitrary collective by excluding others from it. The only universal value being practised as the twenty-first century begins is one that no sensible individual would walk across a street to defend: that the right of post-national corporations to profits circumscribes all other rights. The cathartic aggression of the ethnic and preferential tribes our collective exile is driving us into to lessen our sense of alienation remains subservient to that right.

As recently as a hundred years ago, people in my inherited cultural and political systems experienced life very differently than I do today. Individual and collective life was then set within a tactile complex — an extensive physical community it was possible to be intimate with and knowledgeable about. In that most simple sense, life was "organic." People were figures in and on a stable ground.

For the majority of people who live in North America and Western Europe, and for the wealthy and technology-using classes across the rest of the world, technology has changed this. Yes, it has made life safer, longer lasting, and much less subject to the ravages of biophysical and environmental influences. But the extension of our view and grasp may have exiled us from life itself.

No single, dramatic change nor any single technological advance is responsible, as entrepreneurial futurists are fond of proselytizing. The culprit is the relentless extension and sophistication of our cognitive and technological prostheses. Willy-nilly, and without our consent, they have extended our fields of perception and our grasp so far beyond our tactile perimeters that we easily lose sense that there is anything out there larger and more interesting than near-term human self-interest and ego. This may sound contradictory, but it isn't. As figure subsumes ground, the world — and other people — cease to have meaning.

Only the kids seem to be catching on, as demonstrated by the escalating intensity of the protests against economic globalism over the past few years. Their protests may be clumsily aimed and often without effect, but they're the only politics being waged anywhere on behalf of humanity as a collective, and they're the only politics that presuppose we want a future. The kids are out on the barricades because the twentieth century's noble dreams of world community have been replaced by global monetary racketeering, cultural gang warfare, and mob rule by self-actualizing ninnies in exile from everything but their own navels. They're out there because they recognize that they're being manipulated by multinational corporations and by a financial overclass that has overpowered the civil institutions of the nation state — flawed as those institutions have been.

Activism enables certain kinds of insights, but writers, like other artists, have, I think, a responsibility to pursue something slightly more cerebral. Their job is to script a degree of unmediated and immediate environmental equilibrium and sense, and then play out that script without chewing on the scenery or playing it into a tragic farce for which "others" are to blame. Hence, if I could sweep all the remote controls aside to write and direct a movie about what was important about the twentieth century, it would be about the people and the things I've lived with, amidst, around, atop — and in exile from.

Part of the movie I'd make — the steamrollering high concept designed to entice the interest of production executives and their bankers — would have to be about How Things Fall Apart, How the Centres No Longer Hold. That would be its epic dimension: a technology-infused replaying of the fumbling beast the poet W.B. Yeats sensed at the outskirts of history and civilization in the early years of the twentieth century. Today, anyone can feel that machinery slouching over and through everything worth cherishing about the present and past. Those of us who live in the privileged West live inside its belly, so it is for us, also, the story of Jonah replayed — in which we're not sure if we're Jonah or the Leviathan.

This would be the easiest to script, because it would enact things most people can see and feel if not readily identify: the ribs of the beast pressing in on them, and the sour acidity of its digestive juices. The twentieth century knew more of this than any era since human beings climbed down from the trees and began to walk without scraping their knuckles along the ground. My personal era of consciousness — the decades since, say, 1960 — has experience of the machinery to the exclusion of nearly all else except institutionalized self-aggrandizement and narcissism.

I've just spent twelve years writing a book about how the beast rumbled across the northern British Columbia town where I grew up. But as the book progressed I found myself becoming more interested in the human specifics than the grand abstractions I began by looking for. These specifics were where I regained my surety about what human life ought to be and isn't: a self-mounted struggle to find the fleeting moments where the registration pins align to render immediate accuracies, complex perspectives, and the meaningful lives that might result.

For most of the twelve years I assumed that the book would be about the clear-cutting of the Bowron River valley southeast of Prince George. I began by thinking of the clear-cutting as an environmental atrocity for which the perpetrators ought to be brought to justice — or, at least, skewered by my dazzling prose. As my grasp of the complexities firmed, I began to recognize the clear-cut as the site of an industrial riot, one that is at once typical of the myopic machinery of globalization and a predictable episode in a serial progression of mercantile behaviours that have governed European settlement in western North America. I believed that the rawness and transparency of the way things are here would provide a paradigm of post-modern, post-industrial human behaviour, blah, blah. I guess I also hoped that I could torque my understanding of it sufficiently to be able to demonstrate the velocity and the trajectory of globalization's machinery so clearly that others might see it for what it is — and move to stop it.

I'm not writing this to advertise the skill or accuracy of a book I wrote, though, but to explain exile and why my movie about the twentieth century would make that its central subject. Nor do I think my kindred constitute an oppressed minority or a special case. To make such claims would also make everyone and everything else a potential insult to our group dignity and a possible threat to our group identity. I'm not a special case either. I accept no tribal affiliations, not with my fellow citizens or with other writers. I do live across a continent from where I started, but that's hardly unique or extreme. I've been able to stay within the same nominal culture and language, and I haven't been involuntarily separated from my kin by circumstance or political and social violence. All I am is a well-dressed, well-fed, and extensively if not usefully educated human being a long way from home, with the leisure to think about what that might mean. I'm lucky. But good luck comes with the responsibility to understand other people and places without fear or rancour.

In the past, exile has been a condition from which recovery was possible. Emigrants and immigrants who have successfully recovered from its effects usually employ some combination of ardent citizenship, localized curiosity, and enterprise. Often they bind themselves to a community that shares their condition of geographical and social alienation, and/or to an ethic of diligence and social mutuality. The former protects them from the indifferent or hostile whole, while providing psychological comfort, and the latter gets them ground in the form of physical property.

Since exile means, in the widest sense, figure alienated from ground, then exile is now more or less universal, and my movie would not ask whether exile *is* our condition, but to what degree and depth, and what can be done about it.

The Global Village may be a community of the alienated, but the news isn't all bad. The boundaries of our cognitive neighbourhood have been stretched, but we can use our extended reach to understand that larger zone. To do that we will have to give up the agoraphobia and the xenophobia the stretching has engendered in many of us. Canadian society, in particular, with its multicultural composition, has a chance to become the planet's first mass cosmopolitan society. That would take courage and imagination, and some leadership we haven't had. But the possibility is there. The alienation and loneliness of our collective condition have also raised the beginnings of an instructive animosity toward remote control, and this can be consciously nurtured and educated. A society of the informationally wary is a near-inevitable consequence of globalism's increasingly intrusive totalities. An educated wariness could become the ground for a new kind of social and political wisdom. The figure-to-ground imbalance that is making life confusing and painful can be corrected by specificity and curiosity. As members of collectives and as individuals, we need to sharpen our appetites for both. The alternatives are, literally, unthinkable.

Marshall McLuhan
Twenty Years Later

IN MAY 2000 I ACCEPTED AN INVITATION from the University of Ottawa to investigate Marshall McLuhan's mistakes and oversights at a commemorative conference. I was invited, at least in part, because in the realm of McLuhan studies I have become the troll who lives under the bridge that leads from the information super-highway to the Global Village. That's how one prominent critic described me, and I confess to liking this role, which has been evolv-ing since *Cambodia: A Book for People Who Find Television Too Slow* was published in 1986. One of the episodes in that book had Marshall McLuhan, on the road to Damascus, being kicked by an irritable camel and discussing entrepreneurial technique with St. Paul, and for all the disjunction that deliberately deployed, it was a serious critique of two of McLuhan's weaknesses: his lack of contact with ordinary life, and his "gift" for public relations. Since McLuhan hasn't proved to be a flavour-of-the-week guru, but a thinker who saw far and deep enough into the future to have precipitated elements of it, I had some updated remarks to make about his insights and his errors.

I like my troll job because it doesn't require me to do much beyond what I do naturally: steer clear of official public discourses and the straitjackets of jargon, and keep a watching brief on the real streets and media corridors I live amidst. But as the troll, I've been tossed into the camp of those who are hostile to McLuhan's ideas and approach, or are judged to be unreasonably disturbed by the recent evolution of mass systems.

I *am* disturbed by the recent evolution of mass systems, particularly those related to communications. They seem increasingly shaped and driven simply for financial profits, and run by corporations that are as intellectually complex as reptiles. By contrast, I've always found McLuhan's slapdash style of thinking admirable and curiously efficient — typical of the best qualities of human beings, in other words. In a sense, it is my admiration for McLuhan that has fuelled my concern about the way in which mass systems are being rigged across the human community.

Because I'm not an academic, I have no affiliation with any of the various factions that now ride McLuhan's intellectual slipstream, and I am prone to make fun of these factions without caring about which parcel of his jargon they've fixed on to process. I wasn't lucky enough to have studied under McLuhan in person, much to my regret. But as it happens, I come from what Easterners and Americans are prone to think of as a similar locale — that snowy, Siberian wasteland to the north and west of Toronto. Beyond that, I am, methinks, pretty close to Marshall McLuhan's contrary: a foul-mouthed ex-Protestant atheist who occasionally struggles with bouts of moral earnestness. Despite these differences I have become, in the sanguine sense, more a student of McLuhan than a critic.

It seems to me that Marshall McLuhan was a generally admirable man who could be, if and when occasion and his own character sideswiped him, a jerk. He was a veritable swamp of opinions and beliefs that many people today regard as unpalatable. He was anti-Communist, homophobic, misogynist, and occasionally less than fond of some of his Jewish contemporaries and colleagues without quite being anti-Semitic or anti-Zionist. He thought women were capable of very little ("Women go downhill from the age of twelve"), and he thought most of his students and almost all of his university colleagues were morons. He spewed forth an endless cascade of opinions largely unsupported by facts — but nonetheless filled with perceptive insights and unorthodox ideas. Despite these "faults" in his attitudes and values, there are many things to like and admire about this man, so let's list them.

(1) McLuhan was a first-rate intellectual thief. He was so good at it that it is often difficult to pin down the sources of his key ideas. Among the examples of this is his coining of the term "Global Village," a term central to his entire project, at least in the eyes of the mass media. Did he steal the term from Ezra Pound? Lewis Mumford? Or did he adapt it from Wyndham Lewis's *America and Cosmic Man* (1948), where Lewis writes that "The earth has become one big village, with telephones laid on from one end to the other, and air transport, both speedy and safe."

(2) McLuhan's fame as a talker was matched by his skill as a listener and reader. Consider his insight that media tend to transform the fields in which they operate. Canadian academic Marxists tend to see this notion as a theft from his University of Toronto colleague Harold Innis. But the idea is also a logical projection of Heisenberg's uncertainty principle in physics, of which McLuhan was cognizant. The applicable part of Heisenberg says that measuring a phenomenon changes it, and that the effects of observation and calculation are an integral and sometimes crucial part of phenomenology. I find this particular piece of McLuhan's conceptual assemblage occurring also in American poet Charles Olson's seminal essay on poetics, "Projective Verse," published in 1951. Funny thing. If we go back and do a little investigative work, we find that Olson and McLuhan were in communication during the early 1950s.

(3) McLuhan was a remarkably resourceful and often courageous reprocessor of ideas, an intellectual fabricator, and a compulsive and incorrigible contextualizer.

(4) McLuhan had an admirable gift for what pop psychologists call "lateral thinking," which is to say he is the contrary of computers and corporations. Denizens of the latter found him exotic because his thinking was on the other side of the universe from theirs.

(5) McLuhan is admirable for sticking to his wonderful but unsubstantiated-by-science insight that the low-density images of television scramble the order of perception and information intake. He was, it turns out, right. Neurologists have since discovered

that the neurological effect of scanning a pixel matrix generates alpha waves, which render most people barely capable of critical thought within about twenty minutes.

Beyond these, McLuhan had other, less generally appreciated, qualities I've come to respect and sometimes treasure:

(1) His chronic insolence when faced with institutional bullying and the intellectual cowardice and mediocrity that always lurk beneath it.
(2) His always-evident pleasure at being alive and in possession of a human mind. He loathed anyone who asked him to talk about his feelings and once remarked that he wanted to "study change to gain power over it." By themselves, these constitute an intellectual method the twenty-first century desperately needs to adopt.
(3) His unapologetic generalism, and his desire to see *that* mode of understanding at least stand equal to the specialism and expertism that have swept most of the really interesting cognitive technologies of human civilization straight into the dustbin.
(4) His ability to abandon moral earnestness, which might have crippled him or at least slowed him down to the point where the entropy of academic life would have strangled his wave-motion mode of moving thought along.

But then there's the Global Village, and the things Marshall McLuhan got wrong in defining its promise and its limits. To a certain extent, blaming McLuhan for the Global Village is like blaming the postman for a Dear John letter. He was merely its messenger, a marvellously insightful delivery boy to be sure, of a kind that used to be depicted with winged shoes. But he did not create the world as we now have it, nor was he the Marsha writing the Dear Johns we get more or less daily now from the Global Village. Most of what is ascribed to McLuhan is in our fevered imagination or specious interpretations.

The intellectual industries and the various hagiographic discourses that have grown up around McLuhan and Harold Innis are another matter, and so are many of those who have ridden on McLuhan's intellectual coattails as if they were a magic carpet one must never question the flight quality or airworthiness of. I guess I shouldn't be surprised at academics propagandizing McLuhan and charging fees as high as possible to take elan-seeking corporate sightseers for joy rides. Educated folks need jobs like everyone else and may even deserve to be decently paid for doing them. Still, I won't speak to or within any of these discourses because of their solipsistic nature.

Instead of engaging in hagiography, it's more useful to chronicle some of McLuhan's faults and errors, which I've already admitted to having difficulty distinguishing from his temporary miscalculations and his minor virtues. Hence, I'll list the faults and errors anecdotally, and then try to sort out their effects.

(1) For the ten years between 1955 and roughly 1965, Marshall McLuhan appears to have believed that television was actually going to make people's lives better. Today it is hard to argue seriously that television has improved the active quality of life. It has made for many more immobile lives, yes, and a plague of obese children. Has it also made for less thoughtful lives? I think so. Lives that are more opiated by entertainment? Certainly. Lives communalized only by product-consumption habits and the uncritical ingestion of half-cooked facts? Yes. But it has *not* contributed to lives of superior quality and self-determination, collectively or individually. McLuhan's optimism about television is like his bouts of enthusiasm for Disney and his frequent misidentification of popular culture as a positive political force rather than the neutral sum total of information overload, cybernetic engineering, and mass-market advertising. It was a mistake.

(2) McLuhan's partisanship to his own theories led him, later in his life, to overestimate the pedagogic possibilities of video. This is now a long-standing but still-volatile educational debate inhab-

ited mainly by raucous video education entrepreneurs and, more recently, by the gored oxen of traditional rote teaching. Anyone who has sat through a mind-numbing math class or taken a book-keeping course knows that video and film can be a valuable and cost-saving aid to rote-learning educational situations where the chief issues are how to organize, memorize, and recall data. But video is dead neutral on data interpretation and on how to get along with one another and with our technology while we're reinventing the world.

Even educational television has turned out to be a bitter oxymoron. Learning situations where texture and complexity demand more than simple data input/output require conversation, dispute and discourse, and the "play of ideas" that leads to contextually accurate applications. Ironically, McLuhan's own idiosyncratic pedagogic and discursive habits — about which he may have felt slightly guilty — involve a Zen that simply doesn't translate onto video, as anyone who has seen McLuhan on video will attest. To learn from personal testimony, you have to be there. To teach — and learn — complex subject matters likewise requires physical contact.

Secondary to this, but worth noting, is that video education entrepreneurs have employed many of McLuhan's one-liners outside their intended context and have made him appear more enthusiastic about their cause than he would have been if he'd been asked to consider their specific uses of him and his ideas.

(3) McLuhan's chronic obliviousness to criticism became, particularly in his later years, a tendency to ignore feedback. I understand this was at once a damaging shortcoming and an intellectual strength. The conundrum needs to be pointed out, although I see no way of definitively resolving it. Sometimes it undermined him, other times it kept him from being buried by pedants.

(4) McLuhan's failure to be more circumspect about the retribalization of the world was a damaging oversight. He believed that the dangers of retribalization could be handled by men acting in

good faith, and that the dangers were the result of a lack of organization and good ideas. This view was the product of his Christian optimism, which I'll discuss further along.

(5) McLuhan did us no favour by positing the pernicious notion that the present is going to be reprocessed by the future as its art forms. He did so without bothering to point out that this was only part of how art accumulates and disperses formal energy, an inexcusable error for a James Joyce scholar to make. The notion as relayed by McLuhan was not merely a free insight. It was an incitement to mass-media entrepreneurs, and they've been drowning the public realm in re-warmed art gravy ever since, usually to sell widgets. The present has thereby become the future's raw materials for a nostalgia industry so besotted with messianic commercial enthusiasms that it's no longer clear that the term "art form" will survive much longer without invoking suspicion. McLuhan sometimes mistook "art form" for "profit-generating vehicle," and the consumer corporations pounced.

(6) Similarly, McLuhan didn't do anyone a favour by puffing what are really sensory media tendencies into laws, particularly within a culture where people tend to be overwhelmingly law-abiding. His enthusiasm for codifying things that ought to be treated as dynamic and situational contributed to his celebrity, but it has also been responsible in part for the uncritical public and academic response to the media's flattening and reshaping of human reality over the last fifty years.

(7) McLuhan's passionate defence of his theories has become a posthumous problem because it has given rise to an academic religion within Canadian communications theory no less pernicious than that of contemporary science. In McLuhan's case this is more tragic because his true intentions were to provoke multidisciplinary thinking and to head off the interdisciplinary gang warfare that has become our university system's garden of Gethsemane.

(8) McLuhan's annoying and shameless propensity to suck up to the rich is a fault. Some of his later work was aimed at making his

earlier insights palatable to the corporations and their board-room self-propaganda choirs, which may, in part, be an explanation for the tetrads he was doodling with at the end of his life. The tetrads were probably intended to be corporate boardroom puzzles. More shouldn't be made of this than is relevant, but it shouldn't be forgotten, either. McLuhan was a man who believed, to the end, that the corporate captains he encountered in his travels were *superior beings* when they were merely *specifically focused people*. They occasionally tried to explain this to McLuhan — that they were more entertained by his enthusiasms and unique delivery of ideas than edified by them. He didn't seem to hear it.

(9) Finally, and more seriously, McLuhan's entrepreneurial sense of proprietorship left him unable to recognize that communications are only a *part* of the human puzzle. These days, communications are a very large part of it, but they're not *the* puzzle or even, as Harold Innis was convinced, the cipher to all the other parts.

I don't intend to demean or disparage McLuhan for not having experienced the events of the decades since his death, but it seems worthwhile to point out that McLuhan wasn't a particularly organized thinker, that he was a dreadful empiricist, and that these short-comings had serious effects. Jane Jacobs, likewise a genius, has similar shortcomings. Like McLuhan, she is a fabulous synthesizer and framer of ideas. And, like McLuhan, she's a mediocre researcher.

My most serious misgivings about McLuhan's ideas — and his ideational habits — are rooted in a model he had no way of knowing about. The human genome project, which a few years ago geneticists were arrogantly claiming they'd have mapped and deciphered in no time, turned out to be hundreds or even thousands of times as complex as any geneticist initially calculated. For every affective gene sequence they expected to find there are a hundred or a thousand, each conflated with all the others in an extra-logical matrix. Even these, it now appears, are mixed in with non-sequitur genes that have no decipherable relevance to anything. If we learned anything from the twentieth century it should have been that there is no single cipher to life. And it is not because I'm an atheist that I argue this point. Empirical evidence has been piling up for a hundred years to suggest that life — human and otherwise — is infinitely more complex than hitherto recognized. As a devout Catholic, McLuhan was constitutionally incapable of considering this.

Before I get specific about McLuhan's errors, let me lodge two caveats. First, those of us able to read McLuhan today have had thirty years of additional data on the Global Village that McLuhan didn't have. It is important that we hold him responsible only for what he knew — not for what we now can see.

Second, most of McLuhan's mistakes are the result either of his characteristic carelessness or his too-secure belief in an orderly and ordered cosmos. I realize that in his case "carelessness" is a double-edged term, and one edge helped him to slash through masses of mental algae and other kinds of intellectual and ideological gunk in which our universities were (and still are) mired. His carelessness was a mixed blessing. It gave him velocity, an energy-efficient nonchalance, but it also led to inaccuracies.

McLuhan's belief in order was the product of his Roman Catholic conservatism. It simply does not occur to a man who believes in God and the idea that a physical institution (the church) can be the arbiter of divine revelation that the world can go utterly wrong. That the twentieth century might simply have been a locomotive running at full steam without a transmission, track, or driver was a thought Marshall McLuhan wasn't capable of seriously entertaining.

The global community he envisioned is not a friendly village. It is primarily a fiscal phenomenon organized around the World Bank, the International Monetary Fund (IMF), and the Organization for Economic Cooperation and Development (OECD), all of them organizations with powers that now supersede those of elected governments, and whose narrow goals boil down to protecting the financial portfolios of extremely wealthy North Americans and Europeans. To accomplish this, they are most interested in finding ways to suppress inflation in order to insure that the wealthy retain their wealth and that debtors stay indebted. They want to keep the banking system stable and unreasonably profitable. I don't believe, as some people on the political left do, that these are demonic organizations dedicated to impoverishing the poor and denying them self-determination. I think it is more accurate to say that the financial sector simply doesn't give a damn about the poor and the disadvantaged one way or another.

A few years ago I wrote a book that suggested McLuhan's greatest mistake was not recognizing the Global Village was going to be southern California, specifically Disneyland and Los Angeles. A passage in *Public Eye*, published in 1989 (and since revised slightly), ascribed it this way:

When Marshall McLuhan coined the metaphor of the Global Village to describe the effects massive increases in the volume and speed of information flow were going to have on human individuals and groups, he misread several crucial aspects. Nearly all of his misreadings can be tracked to the same source: McLuhan was a Christian, a Roman Catholic, and he was blinded by the optimism and belief in the essential benevolence of invisible authority inherent in Roman Catholic doctrine and practice — that there is something out there that can forgive mistakes and cruelties. Some of the misreadings, such as thinking that computers would save us from our own stupidity, now seem laughable. But they're typical of a man who believed that if we ourselves weren't able to control our fate, then God would help.

I was right to say, fifteen years ago, that McLuhan misread what the Global Village would be like, but I was wrong about how the Global Village would evolve as we enter the twenty-first century. Since 1989 it has become more a series of fiscal malls than a unified village: London, Tokyo, Milan, Paris, Frankfurt, New York City. The best thing to be said about these malls is that they're impervious to cultural differences and race, which, if you think the first and final aspiration of human life is ownership of a BMW and a diversified investment portfolio, is an advance. While there is now a global financial apparatus and, to a lesser degree, an increasingly standardized international market for commodity exchange and natural resource exploitation, there is nothing resembling a global polity, and no coherent global culture beyond some insincere corporate glorification of independent business, endless enticement to buy and consume products, and, rarely, the same sort of naïve aspiration Woodrow Wilson must have felt in 1918 when, in the fourteenth of his Fourteen Points, he called for the creation of the League of Nations.

Meanwhile, interpersonal, social, and political polity, outside a few enclaves of extreme privilege and wealth, has degenerated into partisan and frequently violent competition over race, ethnicity, gender, and, in the West, sexual and lifestyle preferences. Within that competition, everyone loathes anyone who displays difference or indifference. In North America, where there is sufficient wealth to buffer us from the violence of retribalism, the majority of us get to interact with our preferred institutions and recreational camps while we drift, collectively, towards self-inflicted segregation. At the flashpoints in the world — Kosovo, Somalia, Rwanda, and Palestine — people carry machetes and automatic rifles and suppress differences with flashing blades and flying bullets, just as they did in 1918, except with improved ordnance.

The joyous retribalization McLuhan imagined hasn't produced the vast tribe connected by electronic communications, but, rather, virtually its opposite: a clamour of hostile, competitive, entrepreneurial enclaves competing with one another to gain access to commodities and the dignity they believe possession confers. Culturally, the Global Village of the twenty-first century most resembles the biblical Tower of Babel, with franchise kiosks sprouting from it. This tower is becoming more murderous and fractious as it transforms the constitutional democracies into societies dedicated to the mere accumulation of capital and whatever else the unremitting pursuit of material wealth permits.

Part of this is the evolution of television into a five-hundred-channel universe, and that, like the Internet, wasn't something McLuhan was able to predict. Instead of a unifying, pacifying force that brings a universal language and a new sense of community, television has become the forum within which the emptiness of consumerism meets the competitive violence of tribalism. The unifying mega-network not only did not arrive to bring electronic democracy to the world, but the existing structure of television also broke apart into a chaos of single-focus specialties that allow their corporate funders direct control over the content to a degree of thoroughness Stalin never dreamed of at the height of his tyranny in Soviet Russia.

In the realm of ideas and discourse, our universities have evolved into a vicious state of intellectual tribalism most commonly called interdisciplinary thinking. McLuhan's vision of a global community called for multidisciplinary studies, which would have involved an unprecedented degree of intellectual sincerity and cooperation fuelled by a substance McLuhan himself possessed in abundance, but which is much rarer in others than he imagined: open curiosity.

Here are some of the specific errors I think McLuhan made:

(1) McLuhan didn't foresee the evolution of corporations, even though the corporations were among his most uncritical acolytes and propagandists. There's evidence to suggest that McLuhan, notwithstanding his habit of taking anyone wearing an expensive business suit seriously, thought that the corporations were a lot of small-scale Soviet Unions, albeit with an internal culture much less murderous and threatening. In those days, he was right. But things have changed. The barbarization of corporate culture over the last thirty years is an almost wholly unexamined phenomenon — in no small part because no corporation will fund research on it, and all corporations actively discourage any serious examination from without — or introspection from within.

(2) McLuhan did not understand computers or binary logic despite isolated insights about both. What he did understand of com-

puters — that they might offer us a cosmic consciousness or at least a collective interface with the world — is a misunderstanding of the functioning of the Von Neuman neighbourhood and of how computer-based artificial intelligence construes the world and its contents.

For those who want a detailed discussion of the implications of artificial intelligence, there is a lengthy one in my 1989 book *Public Eye: An Investigation into the Disappearance of the World.* They can also go to the December 1990 issue of *Scientific American,* most of which is devoted to the subject.

Artificial intelligence, or AI, which was a hot topic a decade ago, cooled because most of the AI scientists fled the field. One of the reasons they left was because they discovered that binary AI would be a very *different* sort of intelligence from that exercised by human beings. AI, when achieved, would be capable of vastly superior computational and calculative extrapolation, but extremely limited (even using linked Cray-level supercomputers) in its ability and propensity to contextualize. Ultimately, they found something still more disturbing. Even computing at light speed (as opposed to the 276 miles per hour at which nerve synapses travel through human nerve tissue), AI would lack the ability to experience humour, which turns out to be the most complex of human neurological manoeuvres. One wild-eyed University of California (Davis) AI scientist told me, as he was temporarily leaving the field to study metaphor in Russian literature, that AI won't think we're very funny, and he feared it would, sooner rather than later, try to exterminate us.

(3) McLuhan's understanding of tribalism was inexcusably romantic and naïve. The anthropological record shows that, in isolation, tribal life did have positive communitarian qualities. But that same record also demonstrates that when tribes crowded together, xenophobia and violence became dominant characteristics, and the tribes either morphed into larger social and political formations or degenerated into chaos and perpetual warfare. McLuhan believed that introducing global systems of commu-

nication would precipitate a vast tribe unified by electronic togetherness. The way that tribalism has, in fact, redeveloped shows that most of the old xenophobia and violence reappears with it, and few of the romantic characteristics McLuhan cherished. Many of the renewed ethnic tribalities have armed themselves and are frequently ultraviolent: for example, Rwanda, Somalia, Cambodia, the former Yugoslavia. The "civilized" effects can be witnessed in cities like Vancouver, where official multiculturalism has reduced the city to a nonviolent version of gang and ethnic warfare, with the sub-tribal enclaves squabbling with dysfunctional governments and one another for privileges they would deny to everyone else.

(4) By restricting his working concept of sense biases to the visual and acoustic sensoriums, McLuhan ignored the olfactory bias in human communications, which largely determines fundamental sexual relations between individuals as well as a much greater portion of interpersonal and social life than we care to admit.

Let me illustrate how complex this can get with an anecdote. A few years ago an experiment with mice determined that female mice were more likely to be attracted to genetically dissimilar mice (male or female) before breeding, but that afterward they tended to be drawn to mice with similar genetics (not necessarily those related to them). There was an absolute correlation in this data, and it is sort of obvious why. At the breeding stage, the female mice were extending their gene pool, not because they had any moral objections to incest, but to guarantee the health of their offspring's immune systems — which, it turns out, is what exogamy is designed to achieve for organic groupings of any kind. With an obviously smaller and less credible sample of human females, the same scientists found that women of breeding age, by scent alone, made precisely the same choices when it came to which men they found attractive — unless they were pregnant or on birth control pills, in which case they preferred genetically similar males.

Twenty-five or thirty years ago, a substantial percentage of human females in our culture were choosing their breeding mates while they were on birth control hormones. Ever wonder why there's such a preponderance of allergies and immune-system difficulties among the children born since? Maybe it is the too complex bio-environments, as conventional scientists currently believe — too much pollution overstimulating fragile immune systems. But maybe the hormones we've been putting into our systems are causing us to make erroneous immune-system choices, choices that may have originally been made, as with mice, largely on the basis of olfactory stimuli.

I'd be prepared, at very least, to suggest that the olfactory bias is more effectual than the tactile sensorium, which has done little more than impede the ascendancy of the polyester industry. I won't be making an outrageously Modest Proposal if I suggest that the olfactory bias is as affective as the visual and acoustic biases McLuhan favoured in determining human behaviour. McLuhan also ignored tactility and taste (the latter currently being destroyed by franchise food), both of which remain important components of the human sensorium.

(5) McLuhan didn't see the Internet coming. He can be excused for that, because no one did. How could anyone have foreseen an infinity of five-byte parcels of information, which computer scientists refer to as "Von Neuman neighbourhoods," (a) being transformed by the military intelligence community into a secure dispatch network capable of surviving a nuclear war that takes down 95 percent of existing communications systems, or (b) making 95 percent of existing public communications technologies obsolete, superfluous, and/or ripe for colonization?

Some other transformations that were still in the cocoon when McLuhan was alive have altered the evolution of human society in ways for which he can't be held responsible.

(1) Cellular phone technology and other wireless communication systems. Cell phones have universalized, or rather ubiquitized,

the communications environment, jumping telephones from hot to ultra-cool, and making interpersonal and commercial transactions no longer limited to specific locations. This technology may make life in the Global Village painfully connected and aggravatingly remote at the same time.

(2) In 1986 I suggested that the problem with the Global Village was that its culture too much resembled New York and Los Angeles, and that it was making everything else a suburb — and all but a tiny, ultra-rich elite were becoming alienated suburbanites. Since then, the culture has evolved so that the Global Village in 2003 isn't New York or Los Angeles. It is Wall Street and Rodeo Drive, with the poor outside the gates of both.

I could go on about McLuhan's shortcomings and his mistakes, but there's a point at which minute speculations simply devour themselves, particularly when they're the hard-to-quantify kind I seem to specialize in. When I had lunch with McLuhan's biographer Phil Marchand a while ago, he suggested that I see McLuhan not as a huckster or an Old Testament Jeremiah wailing on the arid hilltops, but as a man in the line of Socrates and the Greek cynics. He liked to talk, and he believed that discourse, not codified pronouncements, was what was important.

That helps. McLuhan is indeed very much like Ezra Pound before him, something of a temperamental village explainer, prone to be wrong as often as right, but willing to stir the pot without fear or rancour because he believed that if the pot is boiling and no one stirs it, the Republic will fail and the stew will be charred at the bottom. Unlike Pound, who thought that the Republic was a series of elevated art *fascistas*, McLuhan believed it could have the commonality and comprehensibility of village life. If we're going to dream, I prefer McLuhan's. His dream was of an intimate democracy where ideas would flourish, and the human mind could expand and be gentled.

Something else, too, this time my own. As I've slowly been turning into an older and more circumspect sort of troll, I've learned to be more grateful for the alternate realities writers and thinkers place me in, and less and less interested when I find them confirming my interests and prejudices. Most often in our era, the realities we're introduced to are depressingly small and confining — a garden here, a dysfunctional family there, a quilting bee here, a jeweller's dais elsewhere. In the company of McLuhan, at least, one is always in or about realities so fast and vast that the danger is disorientation, not sleep-inducing boredom.

Paper Airplanes and Other Alternatives to Gridlock

BACK IN THE 1960S, when the U.S. Congress was holding hearings to consider alternatives to a supersonic transport aircraft (SST) that would compete with Europe's Concorde, a group of Harvard mathematicians submitted a three-hundred-page report offering exquisitely detailed plans for an aerodynamically perfect paper glider. When Congressmen chastised the mathematicians for frivolity, they replied that their paper glider would get people nowhere just as fast as an SST.

I'm not sure if their submission influenced Congress, but the American SST program was cancelled, leaving Britain and France with an open field for the Concorde, an elegant aircraft that has been the costliest, least safe, and most environmentally destructive public transport device ever built. Its sole virtue, beyond its admitted beauty, is that when it crashes it kills only rich people because they're the only ones with enough money and self-importance to fly on it.

The questions the mathematicians were raising, in their slightly abstruse way, have seldom been raised since quite so succinctly. They are also *the* killer questions of the twenty-first century, the ones that the twentieth century ignored, and the ones that lead to almost every practical question that needs to be answered if the human species is not to become a short-lived and fabulously destructive evolutionary dead-end.

Try them out: Where are we going? Why do we need to get there so fast, and what is so important at our destination that we are willing to risk the future of our species and our planet to accelerate our temporal ETAS?

Around the same time that the mathematicians were presenting their SST design, transportation planners made a startling discovery about urban transportation systems that has never been given adequate public airing. It involves an application of what fashionable economists refer to as Say's Law, named after the nineteenth-century French economic mystic Jean-Baptiste Say, who was the first person to suggest that supply creates its own demand. This is the principle that capitalism has been jamming down everyone's throat since the end of the Second World War, and which is now the pseudo-scientific basis for the moral philosophy commonly referred to as monetarism. Stated briefly, the urban planning version of Say's Law posits the idea that all mass-transportation facilities tend towards full use no matter what growth levels are projected for them — provided that the transportation mode used will also speed up average ETAS and permit maximum comfort and passenger privacy.

The specific instance that led planners to conclude that transport supply creates its own demand was a twenty-three-lane freeway built near Atlanta, Georgia. The freeway was built to handle traffic growth for at least twenty years, but three years after it opened, it was running at full capacity. Everyone who could afford a car and a house (more people in those days than now, obviously) simply moved to the suburbs, turning Atlanta's inner city into a combination parking lot and ghetto for poor people and blacks. Most of the city's urban planning initiatives since have been attempts to recover from the effects of building the freeway.

In slightly less spectacular ways, Say's Law was at work all over North America during the 1950s through the mid-1970s, and the problems urban planners are now trying to solve — transportation gridlock, community collapse, strip mallitis, and the untenable suburban land economics that together have made shopping and Prozac the chief amenities of life in the burbs — are side effects of

Say's Law at work. It has also played a major role in creating inner cities that more resemble war zones than places in which human beings can thrive.

Viewed in a slightly different way, all of these phenomena are the result of throwing money and technology at what are really political and cultural choices. Our public officials have been a little like the drunk who some nice sober folk find reeling around under a street-light on a dark night, looking for his lost car keys. When one of the sober folk asks him where he lost the keys, he points down the street into the darkness. Then why is he looking for them under the street-light? It's where the light is.

Yet off in the darkness, Say's Law has an implicit corollary when it comes to urban planning. If no consumption-intensive facilities are provided, people find alternatives to making transportation — which increasingly consists of sitting in gridlocked private vehicles, yakking on cell phones — a primary activity in their economic and cultural lives. Doing nothing, in other words, is often the sanest course of action, and not at all the contradiction in terms it appears.

A Vancouver restaurant owner I used to hang out with once told me that the sign of a healthy body politic was its café culture. If people aren't taking their leisure in public places, he said, and they aren't arguing about what the politicians are and aren't doing, or telling one another stories about what their lives mean and how to make them better, oligarchies take over, and a mix of bullshit and concrete becomes the construction material for human reality.

I'm not sure my friend's theory is always true, or if I'd just like it to be. It's an attractively Socratic notion, and the energy with which the political tyrannies of the twentieth century have tried to obliterate café culture points to its political importance. Certainly the human impulse to sit in the public sunlight and shoot the breeze seems to be strong and resilient, and if exercised diligently by enough people — along with the political right to make smartass remarks — will resist oppression and improve the quality of life more effectively than all the rest of the rights and freedoms we're currently clawing our way over one another to secure. Most of those seem to benefit lawyers and social entrepreneurs more than ordinary citizens, and, these days, some seem to be producing their own special kinds of oppression.

Among the benefits of the shift across the West during the final decades of the last century to market-focused economics and culture has been a reluctant acceptance that people will also go to the marketplace to socialize, and that ideas and stories will inevitably be exchanged. The corporations still want to funnel everyone into the shelf-floor/space cost-benefit formulae their deep-thought drones worship as the pipe to profits, but the last twenty years have, willy-nilly, seen a substantial increase in the amount of small-scale non-dedicated public space, and some recognition that trying to control it is an iffy proposition.

Unfortunately, there's been no significant parallel recognition within the public sector, which has stood stock-still under the street-light, wondering where its car keys might be, while the corporate sector has not only found the keys but has also stolen the car. At least part of the answer to the crucial question of how to make our urban cityscapes and lifestyles ecologically — and psychosocially — sustainable must involve getting planners and the decision-makers who direct them to shift focus from moving people around to creating opportunities for them to stop and stare vacantly into the distances, read a book, chat with the stranger next to them, or do nothing at all.

What I'm suggesting isn't just the not-exactly-hard-to-reach truth that sitting in a running car burning up the non-renewable resources of the future isn't a responsible activity. It's also that we need to get far more creative about our deployment of physical resources, and that we can't go on repeating the twentieth century's error of thinking in too large a scale and too distant a frame. In the twenty-first century, productivity needs a smarter definition. Widget production without any employees may not be as efficient as the right-wing think tanks believe, if only because people without jobs can't buy widgets.

Whether or not multilateral agreements like the Kyoto Accord are empirically justified or politically and economically equitable, the crises they're attempting to address are real. Our resource use and technology deployment is turning the planet into a burned-out toaster. It's not a question of if the toaster will burn out, but when. And we all know it.

The buying and selling of cross-national pollution quotas won't keep the toaster from blackening, and neither will small adjustments to mass-transportation and public energy systems. Looking for natural gas deposits on the floor of B.C.'s Hecate Strait will help only very temporarily, and cleaned-up coal-fired private-sector generation or a new round of doomsday nuclear reactors won't help at all. Net metering, small-scale solar and wind energy-generating systems — I mean the kind that can cover our office buildings instead of shiny plating and glass that do little more than signal the aggressive splendour of this or that corporation — might bring the problem into the context where it belongs: at the level of individual and community responsibility, initiative, and practical real-world choices that have long-range effects on our rapidly vanishing reservoir of resources. The shape of the future, in other words, is locked up inside our heads, or crushed under the weight of our ridiculous expectations — just a synapse away, in the darkness.

Aesthetics and Environmentalism

OVER THE PAST DECADE OR SO, Canadians have witnessed a parade of dramatic confrontations between partisan "interest" groups over environmental issues in British Columbia and elsewhere. It's a safe bet to say that in the next decade we're going to see more, and that some are likely to be more dramatic than anything we've seen so far.

These confrontations are both necessary and inevitable for the simple reason that if we don't clean up our collective act, we won't be here to enjoy this planet much longer. Because I have three children I'd like to see live out their lives without needing to wear gas masks and body suits, I side, whenever I can, with the environmentalists.

Siding with environmentalists doesn't fool me into trusting them or, for that matter, liking them. It's unwise to trust people who believe in purity. It wasn't an accident that the first large social movement to get onside with the Nazis during the 1930s was Germany's environmental movement. Today's environmentalists don't believe in eugenics as a purifying agent, but they have a similar dislike for complexity, and they tend to gravitate toward single-solution focuses like animal rights or virgin forests *über alles*. We now understand that at the core of Hitler's insanity was misanthropy and self-loathing. Far too many of the radical environmentalists I've encountered suffer from something eerily similar.

None of this keeps me from supporting them, because the positions they take on issues are nearly always less self-interested than the ones taken by corporations and governments. Environmentalists may not have a bead on the collective good, but at least they're looking for it.

What bothers me much more specifically is the increasing tendency for the environmental movement to engage in public relations exercises with the corporate sector in which the issues being pursued seem to be chosen on the basis of what can most accurately be called television aesthetics.

The successful campaign waged against the killing of fur seal pups a couple of decades ago, for instance, hinged almost entirely on the fact that fur seal pups are cute. The black-coated, stubble-faced, club-wielding killers spreading red baby blood across the stark white ice floes produced media kinetics vivid enough that about ten minutes of film sealed the industry's fate. Whether the media pageant that ensued has had a happy ending still isn't clear to me — the Newfoundland outports continue to empty of people, and the East Coast fishery, along with the fishermen who insist that fur seals have a taste for cod, is done. What is abundantly clear is this: If those seal pups had resembled Norwegian brown rats or domestic chickens, no one would have cared about them, least of all, I suspect, the environmental issue-pickers.

The controversy in B.C. over the fate of the Carmanah Valley reminded me of the seal hunt. The campaign to save the valley's ancient Sitka spruce trees was launched because the Sitkas of the valley are, well, glamorous and media-attractive, not because the trees are ecologically important or crucial to the fiscal health of the corporation that owned the rights to log them. Sitka spruce are relatively rare in B.C. They're confined to fairly narrow microclimate zones and are famous mainly for providing wood for acoustic guitar bodies and Second World War Mosquito bombers. Beyond that, they don't make any better construction wood than the smaller western white spruce, which are plentiful across the boreal north. That's why the corporation cheerfully gave up its claim on the small area that contained the trees.

What's really significant about the Sitkas is the degree to which they demonstrate that the battle over the environment has changed. The competing propaganda apparatuses were a binary collision of values matched with unanimity of approach. On the pro-environment side, a series of brochures appeared with glamourous full-colour photos of the Sitkas and their mossy eco-niche. A small army of prominent visual artists trekked out to the valley (and presumably through the valley, no doubt tromping all over the fragile flora) with their easels and paint boxes. The coffee-table volume of their artistic sentiments was elegant enough to win a B.C. Book Award in 1990.

The Council of Forest Industries (COFI) responded, with studied indirectness, by mounting Forests Forever, a campaign of slick counterbrochures and television commercials that showed everyone that second-growth forests are beautiful too, and that the forest industry is caring and ecologically responsible — and is working hard to ensure that no one loses his or her job. It was around this time that the provincial government stepped between the two sides and tentatively designated a small portion of the valley as a park. This was soberly judged to be a compromise, and both sides seemed to believe they'd won. But I ain't so sure justice was served or the forests protected.

That's because while the two sides were locked in televised combat over this valley with its picturesque trees, the forest industry remained on the same trajectory it had been on for thirty years, undeterred by the slightly abstract and unpicturesque reality that it is going to run out of trees a couple of decades into the twenty-first century, that its reforestation programs are really just a hodgepodge of overly-optimistic theories, and that the industry has no contingency plan for the looming shortfall other than to shut down and get out.

Common sense tells us that the forest industry won't really change, because it can't. It is governed by short-term profit concerns and by demands of shareholders to keep the profits flowing. Common sense also suggests that the money being spent — on both sides — to keep the media busy and manipulate the public's imagination without disclosing all the facts should be going to research and reforestation. But environmentalists aren't any more interested in common sense than the forest industry. They are content to wage aesthetic battles over small, picturesque parcels of land

and rare animals. That's why, one of these mornings, we're all going to find that our environmental resources have gone the way of the forests of North Africa. There aren't a lot of logging jobs these days in the sub-Sahara. The cute animals are gone too, and the battles being fought there are the kind that only the desert — or Abrams tanks — can win.

Part Two

Why Writers Write

A Reconsideration

ONCE I BELIEVED THAT all writers should write as I do, or rather, the way I *want to* write but mostly don't because my skills fail. I believed, in other words, that there is one right way to write, and innumerable wrong ways.

I've changed my mind. Thirty years of wanting to write the way I'm supposed to and finding that way elusive has mellowed me, even though it doesn't seem to have broken my will. It turns out to be very, very hard to write the way I'm supposed to, and it is hard to write well by any other lights. Good writing, it turns out, is more an event to be celebrated for its rarity than an accomplishment that, once achieved by a writer, becomes a permanent ability. So, since I can't write my writing well on a regular basis, expecting others without my peculiar experience and skill set to do so is unfair and not a little presumptuous. I've likewise given up my belief that there are innumerable wrong ways to write. Instead, there are merely innumerable instances of bad writing.

Mellowing hasn't bred relativism. Instead of a single way to write well, I can see that there are at least six acceptable *motives* for writing. Each can result in good — or bad — writing. More important, each will tend to dictate subject matter and formal consequences, which means that motivation is a primary energy source for intellectual method and personal style.

Some of the motives I'll detail are "legitimate" in that they're expressions of the best impulses human beings have: curiosity, for example. Others are circumstantially unavoidable or physically fundamental to the individual involved, like writing for money and food. Other motives are so compelling for spiritual or emotional reasons that they *seem* fundamental to the writers — and may in fact be so, personally and/or culturally. Others again are seductive, as when something is believed to the exclusion of every other consideration. Each of the six motives requires different cognitive and literary skills, will produce distinct and different artifactual and real-world outcomes, and will let loose characteristic worldviews and cognitive frames in their slipstream and aftertaste. These can be tracked. The job of doing the tracking is one of the things literary criticism and university literature departments ought to do, but don't.

Now, it goes almost without saying that writers aren't motivated by single, fixed impulses, except for very bad writers — or propagandists. Serious writers today must work with mixed motives and an assemblage of research techniques and (increasingly) technologies, most of them now electronic. This simply means that we're writing in the twenty-first century, not the nineteenth, and that real-world rules of engagement tend to reward broadly applied heterodoxy. The alternative is binary logic and the non-contextualizing simple-mindedness of computer-generated corporate writing. People who write business letters, bureaucratic memoranda, and technical manuals are technologists, not writers.

From the beginnings of literature there has been a single constant for good writing: consonance between motive and relevant technique. This consonance has been the best and often sole recipe for writerly success, particularly the worldly kind. At the simplest level, all this means is that it is no accident horror novelist Stephen King doesn't publish a lot of sonnets. He may write them, but that's not what he's there for. He understands genre, and that all genre really ought to define is effective strategies for recurrent situations.

Successful genre writers like King practise a pragmatism that is both native and studied. If you look at King's work with a clinical eye, you'll notice he's not really married to any particular form of expression. What he very much is, is a writer skilled at framing narratives against archetypes reduced to their most elemental contemporary formulation. He will then send the narratives out as movie scripts or whatever other form will net him the largest audience and the most cash. I don't mean this as a criticism. When King exercises his considerable faculties with narratives like *Stand By Me* or *Carrie*, he deserves the public acclaim and wealth he's gotten. He's a great writer.

Now, I'm *not* Stephen King, and because I'm more than mildly agoraphobic I don't aspire to be. But I'm not envious, either. Somewhere along the line I realized that the most remarkable thing about human beings is our ability to produce clear, original thoughts, and that these were, in turn, occasionally able to pierce the fog of bodily and collective life. So I write in order to discover what it is I think, and to then rethink it and articulate my understanding as efficiently and accurately as I'm able. Instead of the "calculate the market/organize/research/execute/package for the market" sequences by which King and others operate, I write in order to rescue whatever it is I'm trying to think from the debris and rubble of unsuccessful thinking — mine and that of others, from bad or fractured ideas and information, from my prejudices, or from stupid psychochemical and physical reactions that could as easily hang from a drooling gibbon as from me.

Like all writers I have an identity, or "self," I generally have to outwit in order to write anything very interesting. My particular self is thickheaded and quite insistent about being the centre of the universe. From a writing point of view this self is annoyingly inefficient and often unpleasant, but it is a comparatively workable one — all I have to do is outwit or outwork the monkey. Other writers I've encountered must cope with selves that are paralyzingly fearful or phobic, or emotionally feckless and precipitate, while others again must struggle with bodies that fail them, either by clamouring for too much attention or by not functioning adequately to allow them the leisure to think and write. I suppose there are a few writers more stupid than I am somewhere out there, along with a tiny minority so clever their giftedness has rendered them idiot savants. I've never actually encountered any other writers who are quite as stupid as I am, and I avoid idiot savants like the plague.

To write by my method, which I can summarize as composing relatively quickly and carelessly and then revising repeatedly until what I started with doesn't sound completely moronic, is a deliberate and labour-intensive process of setting down successive layers of meaning upon an initial insight or idea or group of connected insights and ideas. If the initial materials were genuine, each revision anneals to them a depth of meaning not originally there, and eventually what I've written becomes more intelligent than I could ever hope to be in the immediacy of thought or conversation. When my writing is going well, the textures I can make by revising grow a little richer and deeper with each pass, and the surfaces of the language harder and more faceted.

As the cultural importance of literary writing has faded, I've become progressively more pragmatic about its artifactual purposes. The chance of anything I write surviving longer than a few decades, or — if I'm very, very successful — a few centuries, is small and shrinking. Books on a shelf remain a pleasing sight to me, but that doesn't delude me into thinking that they're important in and of themselves. I just happened to be raised in a print-oriented culture, one in which books were valuable aesthetically and philosophically and were a prime conduit of information. That culture has been collapsing from within and superseded from without by new technologies throughout my life, and books are now considered the least useful and valuable of the many informational commodities thrust at us — even though they haven't lost any great degree of their intellectual credibility. Unfortunately, the idea of "intellectual credibility" has lost much of its social credibility.

But since *thought* is what matters — its temporary and cosmic relevance, its depth of penetration, its originality — to write by my method is accidentally an exemplary political and social procedure that defends me against all the not-thinking moments and temporary commodifications that are now offered as value and meaning. If I no longer practise an influential occupation, I can still have an ethically coherent one, and one that is entertaining and interesting to pursue.

Too many literary writers today seem to believe that thought is tertiary in importance to aesthetic effects, and some of them actually believe that the production of printed (or printable) aesthetic objects is among the intrinsic and ultimate goals of human civilization. This is not only foolish, but also an abrogation of the fundamental miracle of human intelligence. We have consciousness of self and others, and we have language complex enough that we can use it to create social and political — and cognitive — technologies that testify accurately to what we see and understand without falsifying life's miraculous beauty, complexity, and tenuousness. That we are able to manufacture aesthetic commodities out of paper and ink is, by comparison, a puny accomplishment. Print, books, and the culture that surrounds them — pleasant and comforting as they are to people like me — are at most a minor and, technologically speaking, almost certainly temporary expression of that great miracle.

If that makes me appear pessimistic about the future of writing, I assure you I'm not. I'm only pessimistic about our ossified forms of literary expression, along with their shrinking zones of cultural impact. Okay, maybe I'm also pessimistic about writers who treat these temporary expressive formats as if they're the Eternal Verities. At the risk of repeating myself in different words, the deliberate composition of language is, it seems to me, the most complicated action of which human beings are capable. The corollary to this is that poetry is our species' most complicated form of music and mathematics, and the hardest to render with precision and accuracy. If the human species has a future, it will certainly include composed language. In fact, the future will depend on the quality of that composition.

That said, working writers today have to live in the world in which they find themselves, just as they've always had to. For today's writers the world is a very peculiar place. Nearly every human society going is now ruled by its commercial marketplace, a situation that is informationally and socially insane. From there, things gets even wackier. The production of literary writing is to some extent regulated (and in nearly all cases judged) by a class of interpreters and theorists who don't themselves write, know little or nothing about the commercial marketplace, and make a virtue of defending the past of literature against its present and future.

Thus, when I suggest to you that *thought* is more important than art and its artifactual accumulations, I am also lodging a complaint against the formalisms of contemporary university literature programs, whose mission has never been a very convincing one and seems much less convincing today than a few years ago. Establishing the classificatory identity and lineage of a given piece of writing is a solipsistic industrial activity, if not quite the practice of utter fools. With progressive exceptions, literature departments have had their heads so far up their own asses during the last half-century that they have neglected to notice that the marketplace has become the defining instrument of polity. Worse, they have utterly forgotten their fiduciary responsibilities toward the further evolution of human thought.

The impulse to formulate, articulate, and embody ideas is the truly remarkable thing about human beings, not our impulse to classify within arbitrary accounting systems and to accumulate the ossified artifactual remains in storage facilities. Speculative and metaphoric thinking are the most marvellous of cognitive entertainments, and I'm perpetually astonished that only a minority of people, educated or otherwise, seem to understand this. When I first read Joyce Cary's famous remark that no one should feel sorry for artists because they get to spend their days thinking imaginatively and in metaphors about the really important things in life, I knew what *I* wanted to be and do in life.

Finally, I'm aware that there are very talented writers who do not need to proceed as I do to get their writing done. They compose internally, then squirt their sentences onto the page and walk away without further ado. Done, so to speak, in a single pass. At one point in my career I was utterly demoralized by the existence of people who could perform this way. Now I'm just not very interested in them, and if prodded I will point — carefully and respectfully — to the cognitive disabilities their compositional method imposes. Chief among these disabilities is never having the opportunity to overcome their own stupidity by writerly labour, or to experience the joy of getting to the ground of a thought by rooting and scraping at its linguistic and conceptual constituents. Running at my stupidity dozens of times in the course of a normal writing day — and, once or twice a week, winning a temporary respite from it — is vastly more rewarding than the callow satisfactions the single-pass crowd gets. As William Carlos Williams once remarked: "Revise. Something good always comes of it."

So, with that as preface, let me lay out the six legitimate motives I see for writing:

(1) Money
(2) The Record
(3) Ideology
(4) Therapy
(5) The Muses
(6) Curiosity

(1) Writing for Money

Money — needing it or wanting more than one has — is a perfectly acceptable motivation for a writer. Among the different motivators, it has produced more good writing than any other. Dickens and Conrad wrote for money, and so did Shakespeare.

To be successful at writing for money requires a writer to accurately understand who his or her audiences are and to recognize what it is they like to read. In the nineteenth century, Charles Dickens got paid by the word, as did many novelists who serialized their work. This accounts for the often indirect and dispersed narratives of those novels. Subplots are lucrative. If a writer can get his or her audience interested in the difficulties a security guard at a major New York hotel has with removing protruding nose hairs while other characters in the same story are trying to detonate a stolen H-bomb in the parking garage, *ka-ching!* These are Dickensian strategies, designed for an era when killing time was the major purpose of fiction, along with teaching people to read and filling their heads full of the sort of nonsense that accidentally propagandized the interests of the ruling class — or, more rarely, tickled the fancy of the writer.

Then there is William Shakespeare, who may be unique in the history of writing in that he wrote for all the classes of his society and managed to get and keep them all interested in what was taking place on his stages. We hear about Shakespeare's wordsmithing skills *ad nauseam*, and such talk hides a more important truth that is the source of his greatness. He knew his world well enough and was comfortable enough in it that his creations appealed to his entire society. No other writer has accomplished this.

In our era, writing skillfully and seriously *and* for money requires that the writer understand the marketplace far better than most do, and it also demands an unusually strong moral and intellectual constitution. Another asset is a relatively low level of self-involvement. It is no accident that when Stephen King was hit by a car several years ago and almost killed, he wrote about the driver of the car, the people who rescued him, and the people in the hospital before it occurred to him to be interested in his own near-death reactions.

Please note: (1) If all you care about is making money, it is easier and much more lucrative to write real-estate contracts, ad copy, or stock-market buy/sell orders. (2) *You* can't be Stephen King, so his technique can only be your gimmicks — and gimmicks never work.

What do I mean by that? Well, during the time I spent teaching writing in maximum security prisons, I was pestered constantly by my students to reveal the tricks of the trade. I told them that writers like Stephen King or even old Charles Dickens didn't become famous because they used gimmicks and tricks. They were lucky, yes, that their peculiar set of skills and interests coincided with public needs and tastes. But much more important was that those writers knew their own strengths and limitations, and that they worked hard. Successful writing — of any kind — means writing every day pretty much the way normal people breathe, and doing enough research on whatever you write about that you no longer think of it as "research." I still believe that.

(2) *Writing for the Record*

It is a post-modern taken-for-granted to suppose that history is dead and over, and that there is nothing left but jewellery design and self-involvement of one reeking sort or another. Among the most damaging penalties of the post-modern condition is the one many writers revel in: a pervasive sense that progressive time has ended and that history — perhaps particularly the history of ideas — is simultaneous, relative, truthless, and open to entrepreneurial manipulation. Admittedly, there are considerable advantages to the intellectual buffet post-modernism confers on us. One can, in the twenty-first century, as easily be a student of Heraclitus as of Milton Friedman or today's version of yesterday's Bagwan or Marshall Applewhite. I'd need a book's length to argue the many hazards of this, but I'll settle for reminding you of how your last buffet-style meal tasted. And I do want to specifically address one hazard that writers can do something about.

With the collapse of historical consciousness, personal journal-keeping has fallen into disuse, and I mean the kind of journal-keeping in which people regularly write down their impressions of what it is they see, hear, smell, and touch. People today, including many writers, don't think life is worth recording because we're at the centre of time and at its end. What's the use?

The public danger in not keeping these records is substantial and simple. We're about to leave an information gap for those who come after us that will be irreparable. Fifty or a hundred years from now, no one will know what it was we are seeing and thinking today. This is doubly dangerous because electronic technologies have destroyed the world of exact and verifiable documentary evidence — a world that commenced during the 1850s with the advent of photography and ended about a decade ago when commonly available technology and software made it possible to transfer the head of George W. Bush onto the shoulders of a barnyard animal or Albert Einstein. In such a world, personal testimony must take the place of what was documentary, because no document can any longer be definitively authenticated. Yet as our faith in documentary evidence crumbles, we are ceasing to testify to what is happening around us in other ways. This will leave the writers of the next generation without the database that today's writers enjoy.

Perhaps the most crucial function of writing in the twenty-first century, then, will be the one we see as the least important today: keeping accurate records and making laconic descriptions of the world around us. If we don't do that, there will be no immediate past for the next generation.

(3) Writing by Ideology

Very few people today, writers or not, have an adequate understanding of the degree to which they and what gets written by them are determined by ideology. Ideology need not be professed in order to be the controlling force in a piece of writing or in a life-project. The most common ideological determinant today when it comes to writing is the one that is most rarely acknowledged: the idea that whatever one is doing — art, social advocacy, community development — is not political because it is right, just, and correct. Conflating political fact with polemic content is stupid, because all writing has political content. Those who argue for the apoliticality of writing are merely making a clumsy defence of some element of the status quo they either don't recognize or have reason to make obscure to others.

By ideology I mean something quite specific: a moral or intellectual value system imposed on phenomena as received truth or infused into the body of imaginative work clandestinely as subliminal messaging. It was once called "common knowledge," but the conditions for cultural unanimity have not existed since the time of Martin Luther in the sixteenth century. Generally speaking, we've been better off without common knowledge because it breeds authoritarian and totalitarian notions. Its eclipse has permitted the flowering of knowledge and free inquiry over the last four hundred years. The various outbreaks of imposed cultural unanimity in the twentieth century — Soviet and Chinese Communism, Nazi-Fascism, and many of the recent outbreaks of exclusionary tribal, ethnic, or preferential nationalism — have been uniquely lethal and may be trying to tell us how much better off we are without it.

This is because ideology is the inevitable repository for — and energy source of — all the processes that are inimical to free inquiry and expression. Ideology is also dedicated to the subjugation and controlling of consciousness and is therefore inimical to the fundamental purpose of art, which is to liberate the human mind from whatever happens to be encumbering its attempts to entertain the mind and educate the body. Ideology today is a greater danger to writers than it was a generation ago, when the global movement toward secularized skepticism was at its too-brief apogee. In case you haven't noticed, we're now in a headlong retreat from that skepticism into fundamental and sectarian beliefs.

There is a naïve tendency among writers to equate ideology with propaganda and dismiss both as vulgarities of little concern. This causes them to ignore a fundamental change in the relationship between ideology and propaganda, and the subtle shifts in form it has taken. In a strict sense, propaganda, which Cyril Connolly usefully defined during the 1940s as the "genial undermining of truth and beauty by the State," has become relatively rare in the West now that multinational corporations have overpowered the state in virtually all terms of effective power. Commercial advertising has far outstripped government propaganda as a determinant of both the public realm and individual consciousness.

Any examination of the evolution of corporate advertising in the last thirty years reveals the visible effects of this transformation. A startling percentage of today's advertising no longer pitches the virtues of a specific product, but rather is aimed at making the corporation palatable or heroic. Structurally, advertising is aimed at occupying media space. This has two effects: (a) It buys the attention of the media — in a literal sense — i.e., the corporations are paying their bills by buying advertising from the media companies, and (b) It occupies the attentions of the public while ensuring that others don't. In an era obsessed by information, media space constitutes a new type of totality that is historically unique. It contains no silence or absences, and since the corporations have no interest in, or responsibilities to, public well-being and individual privacy, it focuses attention almost entirely on commodity exchange. Thus, whatever portion of the space is occupied by a given entity constitutes real control of that portion of public attention, since media space and the public realm are informationally the same thing.

Because it is schooled by corporate advertising and shares the same willingness to engage in self-interested cognitive obscuration, today's ideological writing is more subtle than the committed writing of the past, tending to separate itself from its implications and gestalt without its authors' full awareness. You'll hear writers suggesting, subtly or not, that what their enemies and opponents posit as value is propaganda, whereas their own claims are analytical and "true." An extremely simple way to sort out the new dimensions of propaganda would be to treat anything articulated from received truth as different from old-style church or state propaganda only in its surface rhetoric.

Thus, in a corporate-determined (if not formally governed) cybernalia, business writing and feminist writing are basically the same because the cosmological attributes attached to them are determined before the phenomenal elements are treated, and will ultimately govern the latter's selection.

Now, I'm not suggesting that good writing can't come from a socially or politically committed writer. Many of the great writers of the nineteenth and twentieth centuries — Emile Zola, Ignacio Silone, Charles Dickens, or John Steinbeck — were committed to various aspects of social justice. The list of competent politically committed writers is an absurdly long one, and if I name any more it will be an unproductively contentious list, and one that betrays my intention. The difference between most of the writers who have survived their own time and many of today's committed writers is that the old writers had a clearer idea of the limits that need to be placed on ideological commitment. It is one thing to be committed to some idea or cause, another thing to be partisan to it. Partisans are prone to shoot people they think are getting in the way of their cause. This isn't a very good way to get art done, and it is a very bad way to get your work remembered. Good writing must transcend orders-of-the-day, however hot and seductive they seem in the urgent ecstasies of the moment. At a basic level, this is a variation of the old "Don't run with the scissors, kids!" with pen or laptop computer substituted for scissors. You may be more likely to damage the technology than injure your physical person if you fall, but don't make the mistake of thinking that the damage won't get you. Information technology is cognitively prosthetic and as essential to survival as wrists, ankles, lower intestines, and the more commonly mentioned appendages.

Ideologically determined writing can be a legitimate form of human expression. But writers with an overly confident sense of what is good and what is evil are almost always bad writers and thus almost never survive their own moment in time. In our time, the term "activist-writer" is very close to an oxymoron.

(4) Writing as Therapy

Therapy gets a bad rap from writers, and not always for just cause. There are reasons for the bad rap, of course. Self-therapy by and of itself is contentless the same way the self is without content when separated from knowledge and other people. Additionally, in a market-obsessed culture, interactive and/or group therapies fail because they get hijacked by the therapists' need to develop profitable clienteles or to hold onto them once developed. Therapeutic processes, in other words, too often end up in the service of the therapists. (Sometimes, of course, therapy gets a bad rap simply because therapy-heads deserve to be made fun of.)

Most writers have forgotten that nearly all of us first put pen to paper because we wanted to explain to ourselves some ineffable or confusing real-world circumstance or consequence impenetrable by conventional means of assimilating (or dismissing) experience. Understanding is therapeutic, whether we leave it there or not.

I first began to write, for instance, at the age of sixteen when my friends decided to punish a disliked junior high school teacher by killing a stray cat and hanging it over the teacher's door. During those years, this wasn't nearly the outrage it would be today. But for reasons I was completely unable to explain to my friends or understand for myself, I couldn't join them. They went out and did the deed, and I stayed home. But staying away wasn't quite enough. I needed an explanation, not of the cat-killing but of my refusal to participate. I found some paper and a pen and sat down at the kitchen table. Before long I'd written a very bad (and mercifully soon lost) poem.

I felt no moral superiority because of my pacifism, then or now. At the time, what I did was instinct, and I rather feared it was a shameful one. From writing the poem I discovered that my instinct had not in fact been shameful, and that stepping away from the dynamics of social life could be an honourable course. There was more to it than honour, too. In the moment of that first composition I experienced the deepest pleasure I had known to that point in my life. I was thinking, and I was exercising my independent will, and I was finding the best way to substantiate those with words. I wanted to spend my life doing it.

Other pleasures have since succeeded that moment in intensity and depth: parental and romantic love, for instance. There have also been one or two culinary and aesthetic experiences that have matched it, and many moments of reading have been in the range. But I became a complete human being by writing that first time, albeit a particular and maybe peculiar kind of human being: often solitary, usually independent, but determined to be the investigating messenger of everything that was not me, but which I could discover — or build — a bridge to. For me, to write is to become fully human.

I suspect that nearly all writers begin writing so they can understand themselves or explain some important personal or historical event, circumstance, or stress obscured by everyday living. The process of writing is in and of itself illuminative, and even the most professional and experienced writers retain an element of that beginning in their work. Whether they admit it — or are even aware of it — many writers spend their lives using their writing to explicate or purge personal traumas, or to transcend perceived disabilities or inflicted disservices and injustices. But problems arise when the rhetoric of therapy invades a writer's motivation and makes the writing itself responsible not to the technical demands of art — clarity of articulation, the embracing and celebration of complexity and accuracy — but to the therapeutic needs of the author.

Let me offer an anecdote to illustrate what I mean. Several years ago I became the unpaid editor and counsellor to a young lesbian who was trying to come to terms with her mother's impending death and, not incidentally, with her mother's refusal to accept her sexual preferences. I encouraged the young woman to document her mother's last days and to use the role of observer to try to get beyond the long-standing hostilities to some sort of mutual closure. She did this, with some positive results, making tape-recordings of her last conversations with her mother. After her mother's death, I suggested that she could get a stronger understanding of what had happened by writing about it.

Eventually, the young woman did move past recordings and journals and began to write stories. At first I welcomed them because I thought it would offer her a chance to make her parents real to her in ways they'd failed to be in life. But from the first, the stories she showed me were slow-moving and devoid of substantive action or insight. The characters she modelled on her parents were without any seeming capacity and purpose other than that of explaining their future hurtful behaviour towards the story-author, their daughter. Both stories and characters were drab and intransitive, capable only of a depressingly inexorable descent into the exact conditions under which their author's parents ended their lives.

When I objected to the turgidity and the self-serving distortions, the young woman argued that the events depicted in the stories were "real," and that the stories were therefore "true." I hung lugubrious quotation marks around the words "real" and "true," but she didn't crack a smile. I offered her Audrey Thomas's useful dictum about how real-world verities don't excuse bad architecture in fiction, and then, more gently, suggested that as a young writer she needed to be, as Kurt Vonnegut has it, a good date on a blind date, and generally try to "show strangers a good time." When she accused me of being callous with her feelings, I replied that when a relationship involved writing, my priorities are to make the writing readable, and that everything else, including tender authorial feelings, slips well down the list.

She wasn't able to hear any of this. I don't know exactly why, but it's reasonable to assume that she was more interested in feeling better about herself — in this case by confirming her victimhood and alienation from the smothering normality of her parents — than in making readable stories. That's a perfectly acceptable life choice, but it is one that ensures that, once made, you won't be much of a writer. In order to succeed — however we define success — writers must learn to gain and keep control over their neuroses, at least for the purposes of writing. I remain prepared to go the distance on the point that, among writers, better prose is more important than stroked feelings.

Having said that, contemporary writers *could* use their skills for purposes other than creating good sentences and technically sound fictions. There exists a void in our, er, Mental Health Procurement Apparatuses that writers — perhaps particularly fiction writers — could easily fill, and with powerful effect. It involves storytelling and helping others who don't have the skills writers have at refining stories.

What writers know about telling stories may be, in the end, the most important social skill they possess. No, don't laugh. If I were setting down what I think are the basic needs of a human being today, I would list food, shelter, tactile contact with others, and some measure of social and political justice, pretty much in that order. Right after that — before the need to get laid, actually — I would put the need to know where one's life has been, where it is set, where one stands in the complex continuums we all inhabit, and where one would like to be in the future or in an ideal world: in other words, the need to have an understandable life story.

People who don't know their own stories are common today and getting more so. The skills of narrative-making are often among the first casualties of the speed and provisional nature of contemporary life — and of contemporary mass media, which tends to break individual experience down into atomized parcels that are inexorably drawn in the direction of the nearest market check-out station. It's one of the rarely recognized costs of living fat in a safe world.

I had this driven home to me recently by a friend — not a writer — who was in the throes of a nasty divorce. He complained to me one afternoon that the lawyer he'd hired wasn't having much success defending his interests. As he described what had been happening, it came to me that the reason the lawyer couldn't serve his case was because my friend had become so scrambled with the collapse of his domestic life that he no longer *knew* his own story or his position in the world in relation to those around him. He was therefore unable to define either his interests or his intentions — to his lawyer or to anyone else.

Over the three weeks that followed his confession, I used the skills I've accumulated as a fiction writer to help him construct a written version of the events of his decade-long marriage — its "storyline," as it were. I began by getting a bare-bones structure of names and dates from him, which I wrote up as a first-person narrative, one that contained several deliberate misinterpretations designed to get his attention focused on the virtues of getting the story right. From there, I convinced him to read and revise it until it was fleshed out into a connected net of events others could follow. As his story rounded slowly into coherence, I saw my friend, for the first time, come to terms with what had taken place since the marriage fell apart. As he did, I saw his anxieties fade. When the narrative was complete and he'd read it over a few times, he took it off to his lawyer, and the divorce began to proceed — not happily, but at least without the crippling effects it had been having on him.

Now, doing this for him wasn't a big drain on my time, and the writing part of it was easy because I was aiming only at narrative coherence, not artful language. But its effect on him and his life was disproportionately large, and it made me consider whether this sort of narrative-making is a service professional writers should be offering to non-writers more generally and generously than they do. It would likely be a highly effective therapy for a number of contemporary psychological predicaments. As writerly jobs go, it wouldn't be quite as exciting as transcribing the dictums of burning bushes onto stone tablets on a mountainside, but it is decent work, and the kind that will diminish the general misery of our stupid lives.

If you pinch me hard, I'll still tell you that therapy by and for its own sake doesn't work, and that writers had better not be writing merely to make themselves feel jingle-jangle and warm down below the waist or between their ears. But now I'll add that none of that should prevent writers from employing their narrative-making skills to help people who don't have those skills themselves.

(5) Writing for The Muses

Every poet once knew who the Muses were. In classical Greece there were just nine of them, and they're still worth naming: Calliope for epic, Clio for history, Erato for lyric poetry, Euterpe for flute, Melpomene for tragedy, Thalia for comedy, Polymnia for church music, Terpsichore for the tango, and Urania for astronomy. Today there are many more Muses around because the human part of the world is much more complicated. These new Muses rarely stay within the categories by which the Greeks understood reality. A few of the original ones have changed — like Polymnia, who's now doing techno-rock at raves, and Euterpe, who's catatonic in an institution somewhere, suffering from Kenny G and Zamfir overload. Urania writes her own astrology column at *USA Today*, etc.

I could amuse myself this way more or less indefinitely by adding and subtracting Muses, but the Muses are not a parlour game, and they aren't antique or obsolete. They are, today as in the past, externalizing agents for identifying and channelling the obsessive energies without which writers can't get anything done. That's why it might be a useful exercise for writers to gain an understanding of who and what the Muses were to the ancient poets, and how they can help writers today to gain and hold perspective on themselves and the subject matters they are best suited to pursue. Most of today's organizing icons are narcissistic personifications of aspects of career and private projections: the Entrepreneur, the Earth Mother, the Captain of Industry, the Female Pioneer, the Lover, the Warrior Prince or Princess. These are fine for pursuits that require heavy doses of egomania to thrive in, but utterly distracting if you're lining up the registration pins on the most exacting details life gives up.

To be a writer is to be occupationally schizoid — or, to use T.S. Eliot's distinction, to live with a permanent separation between the person who observes and writes, and the person who acts and feels and is acted upon. The Muses, in effect, are the anchors within the experiencing identity that reminds those of us who write that, for us, life is about writing, not about us — or at least not *merely* about us. To embody that permanent reminder that we are not our own is a convenience that involves a piece of trickery of which we are at once the victims and proprietors. To be openly both will bother few serious writers because the dualities are already familiar whether we acknowledge them or not.

In the last two centuries, the Muses have been collectivized by Stendhal as *The Happy Few*, conflated with the history of music and poetry by Robert Graves as *The White Goddess*, or abstracted to what Mayakovsky called *The Social Command*. Each of these distinctions is educative, but no longer entirely accurate. The Muses have also been understood as The People, or the General or Reading Public — although it is as hard to find a constituency that recognizes those collectivities today as it is to locate Mayakovsky's ghost.

Since the Second World War, the Muses have occasionally taken the form of cataclysmic life experiences that rearrange one's sensorium or moral apparatuses. For Kurt Vonnegut it was being captured by the Germans during the Battle of the Bulge in late 1944, which put him in Dresden in 1945 for the massive Allied air raid that created a firestorm and burned the city to ashes — along with all of Vonnegut's preconceptions about the human condition. For Primo Levi and Paul Celan it was the Nazi death camps. For Albert Camus it remained the city of his birth, Algiers, or for Dorothy Parker, more minimally, a table in a New York restaurant.

The form my private Muses took was more personal and less profound than even Dorothy Parker's. They showed up while I was sitting solemnly in a coal shed at the age of three while my family frantically searched for me in the bright world outside. This four-hour experience was so inexplicably ecstatic that it has had me since permanently peering out at the world through a slight, dark, but always intervening reserve that the world's overwhelming but seductive violence perpetually seeks to invade.

More than any other class of fools the twentieth century and its ideological steamrollers have flattened into dictatorships — be it of the Proletariat, Entrepreneurs, or Self-Involved Middle-Class Ninnies. Artists and writers have been cheated of a large part of their cultural birthright by remaining ignorant of what the Muses actually do. The poet we now call Homer didn't get his vision of the string of bonfires stretching from Troy to Mycenae to signal the end of the war and the beginning of a new world by gazing at a campfire or holding hands in a tribal circle. He — or she, because there's powerful evidence to suggest that Homer was a woman — saw it from the hilltops outside the city, or from the roof of Agamemnon's palace. Homer was of the city and of the people, but he or she was not *with* either, physically or spiritually. The ability of any given writer to identify and seek out that specific but never total isolation from the whole defines the Muses.

Awareness of the Muses is one thing, consciously writing for them another. In our era, perhaps as a reaction to the sheer force and pervasiveness of the governing systems around us, self-conscious writing for the Muses tends to express itself in a narrower-than-it-looks formal and behavioural band that ranges from non- or anti-commercial obsession to exemplary political and social activities. Some are poets, but not all. For many writers, the fun is over by the time a book goes to press, or a poem to performance.

Despite my agoraphobia, performance anxieties are fairly temporary and minor distractions. This isn't because I've made myself a good performer. It's more that I don't take it very seriously because it now has so little effect beyond sales and social prestige, and because I get so much more pleasure from reading, writing, and revising.

As I've grown more solitary, I've lost much of the interest I once had in tracking the psycho-kinetics of writing — my own and those of other writers. I get my real pleasure from the construction of precision. I trained myself to sever contact with the Muses for months at a time in order to suppress the obsessive elements of my personality, opting instead to generate writing from conventional research activities. The logic behind this trick is completely pedestrian. If I can't use the research for writing, at least I'll know something more than I did before I started, and what I'll know won't be my feelings about myself.

I wouldn't go so far as to make a blanket recommendation for this approach. Every writer needs to find the most productive ways to relate to the Muses. Standing at a slight and darkened remove, remember, is a private instinct, and the Muses themselves aren't excluded. But losing touch with them altogether creates as many dangers as letting them run your life. Ignoring them pisses them off, and they're no fun when they turn on you. Who says it has to be nothingness or blood pudding?

(6) Writing from Curiosity

This is the cleanest motive I can think of for writing, for the simple reason that the more a writer knows, the less likely he or she is to resort to arbitrary beliefs or faith. I've noticed, as I get older and biology becomes progressively less intrusive and demanding, that I'm becoming more rather than less curious. I'm curious about how the human world works and why it doesn't, about what's unique in it. When I'm depressed, I'm curious about how much longer the human species can keep on using nature as its rationale for every screwup before we're removed by the planetary biological collapse that will result if we don't start taking responsibility for our intelligence. It's worth noting that attempts to formalize writerly curiosity usually seem to fail. The curiosity of some writers dies as they get older, and that makes them into old dogs doing old tricks. Since the inherent heterodoxy of art makes it the perfect tool for investigating a world that has become otherwise almost intolerably complex, that's a shame — and a curiosity.

I've noted that writers who seem to be the most happy in old age tend to have cultivated their curiosity the most assiduously. That's because curiosity is a better and more clean-burning fuel than testosterone, dedication to a cause, ambition and lust, or the fear of failure.

I don't see much need to apologize for the sort of curiosity I exercise and the peculiar way it operates. It has become so thoroughly integrated with my personality I can't separate it from who I am. A writer's curiosity has little of the coldness of its empirical cousin — or it is a different sort of coldness — and if it sometimes also involves experimentation on living beings, both the experiments and the animals so used are metaphorical, and so are the electrodes that get attached. Among the benefits of the descent of writing into cultural and political unimportance is that it encourages curiosity. Douglas Coupland's *Generation X* hasn't had the range and kind of impact of *A Christmas Carol*, which single-handedly created Christmas as we practise it today with its Peace-On-Earth-Good-Will-To-Men theme. Today, works of literature can no longer be expected to reshape social or cultural institutions, stop massacres, or change the face of war. But they're also unlikely to convince people to kill others. What remains, after the acclaim has faded, are the luminous traceries anything good leaves in the world. For today's writers, that may be the only permanence we can leave behind.

Depressing? A little. But therein lies a small but brilliant freedom that the commercial cropping of genre literature has clouded for most of today's writers. We can take the leash off our deepest curiosities. The indifferent liberty of twenty-first-century writers is a more or less direct incitement to curiosity, and perhaps (I can never quite resist a manifesto opportunity) a responsibility. If one's writing has no influence on the political centre or the marketplace, it becomes the logical instrument for exploring the margins and the obscure but chemically active back-eddies. If one is no longer at the centre of human culture, one can claw at the palace doors hoping for re-entry, or one can go off and explore the far shores of the realm. The third alternative, industrial production, isn't a terribly attractive or serious one. I'd sooner find a factory and manufacture widgets or something else that'll make me rich while it's rendering me terminally dull.

By the way, this list of motives is not exhaustive, merely relevant and sufficient. There might be other reasons for writing. One writer suggested "love" and "revenge." Another offered "life itself," i.e., our evolved biological condition, as adequate grounds. Practitioners of the trade are invited to add their own.

Finally, an addendum about why writers fail, because most do.

(1) Not writing. Insufficient time spent with pen against paper — or fingers against plastic keyboard squares — is the surest way to end up as something other than a writer. Windups don't count as writing, and neither does lab work, unless you're a poet

with a high tolerance for drugs and booze and aren't very distracted by sex. None of the excuses for not writing, however
compelling or sincere or elegantly posited, count as writing.
Writers are people who write. If they don't, they're not writers.

(2) Insufficient attention paid to the audience for writing. Most
writers, including many who achieve technical competence,
make exaggerated estimates of how many people are readers
and have unrealistic notions about what those who do read are
interested in reading about. Almost all writers, according to
Stephen King, are oblivious to the issue of audience interest,
and he believes much of the misery of failed writers can be
traced back to this. I agree.

(3) Technical interferences. The first and second reasons above
often require a chemical reaction with a site-specific factor to
actively prevent writers from working. Below is a list of possible
site-specific factors, in no particular order:

(a) Lack of skills

(b) Lack of talent (They're different)

(c) Children

(d) Shifting markets for written products

(e) Technology screwups (In the word-processing age, most writers lose anywhere from two weeks to two months a year to
technological "innovations" of one sort or another — new
machines, new software, hardware catastrophe, etc.)

(f) Market capitalism seeking the lowest common denominator, a
point to which no writer willingly — or at least knowingly —
wants to work towards or on behalf of

(g) Sex, Drugs & Rock'n'Roll (A particular favourite of most
poets)

(h) Lack of ruthlessness

(i) Lack of concentration

(j) Insufficient laughter while working

(k) Disappearance of publishers (This is a current difficulty in
Canada, and one that is likely to get worse)

My own nemeses tend to be factors (h) and (i), although earlier in my career I was a frequent victim of (j). Even so, I noticed that if I didn't get myself past the first two reasons for failing, subsequent ones never much mattered. At that point they're excuses, and excuses don't produce writing.

Richler's End

MORDECAI RICHLER'S DEATH in July 2001 deprived Canada of its premier male novelist, and Quebec nationalism of its most insightful — and irksome — political critic. This is a serious cultural loss because Richler was a fine novelist, one whose last novel, *Barney's Version*, might have been his best. Certainly he was in command of his powers when he died. The bulbs were all lit, and the wattage undiminished. Timothy Findley, who was, with Stephen Vizinczey, the only other Canadian of Richler's generation with the talent to get within barking distance, had been headed in the opposite direction with the three novels that preceded his death eleven months after Richler's. The best of Findley's last novels, *Headhunter*, managed just a single galvanizing chapter — the first — before descending into bathos and florid descriptions of Rosedale manners. Vizinczey has been silent for almost two decades, and his remarkable first novel, *In Praise of Older Women*, was, like Findley's *The Wars*, his finest work. These sorts of trajectories are more common than the one Richler was on. In that sense, among the more sentimental ones, it is worth noting that Richler's death at the age of seventy was premature and even tragic.

An examination of *Barney's Version* bears that out. At four hundred pages, it is not the slight book of a failing mind. Nor is its central character, Barney Panofsky, a man earnestly sorting his doilies and quilts as the Grim Reaper approaches. He's a wealthy schlock-television producer in the early stages of Alzheimer's, still fighting his way through the mess of life: three ex-wives, three children, a trail of wreckage that includes emptied tanker-trucks of scotch, innumerable polluting cigars, a raft of alcoholic cronies, and the possible murder, long ago, of a close friend. The Alzheimer's hasn't created this mess. Panofsky has, and his failing neurons merely make the puzzle more baffling. The memory lapses everyone manufactures are, for him, involuntary — and occasionally hilarious.

But Panofsky, like Richler himself at the end of his life, is more interested in kicking holes in his tent than in folding it, and silence isn't an option. Panofsky isn't always likeable — he's as grouchy and irascible as Richler himself often was, but his gallows-humour bickering is wildly entertaining and believable because it pokes satirical holes in both the object of Panofsky's ire — the wilderness of human vanity — and himself. It is also deeply moving, because beneath it are penetrating whispers about what life comes down to at the bottom of the night. Those whispers aren't exactly common in recent literature, least of all in our own literature, where the older writers tend to grow florid and magisterial as their faculties fade.

Barney's Version is, by the way, unapologetically Canadian. Panofsky is a Montrealer, and the setting is anglophone Montreal during the 1995 Quebec referendum, on the subject of which Richler's character is almost as wrathfully insightful as Richler himself was while it was happening, albeit far more over-the-top. Panofsky is both Richler himself and his contrary dark side, and, one suspects, a creation that Richler enjoyed immensely — and was terrified by. Panofsky's grouchy, abusive cantankerousness is Richler himself without the inner moral centre. His depiction of Miriam, Panofsky's third wife, grand passion, and lost real-world compass, has a poignant autobiographical parallel. You get the sense, through the chugging and pratfalls, that this is an unsentimental love poem to Richler's own beloved wife, for whom he organized his life to avoid Panofsky's fate.

The deeper you get into *Barney's Version*, in other words, the larger and more complex the canvas he's working becomes. Only American novelist Philip Roth, among his contemporaries, has Richler's degree of control and daring. That said, where Richler's reputation will settle outside Canada is hard to gauge, as is the trickier issue of how important novelists and novels are going to be in the culture of the twenty-first century. Novels remain fashionable within the book-publishing sector mainly because the mass media find them easy to process, and because they sometimes pay off handsomely in movie rights. But they're not, methinks, very important, commercially or cognitively, in the larger framework where we make our judgments about what is good, bad, survivable, or a road to the future.

Not that you could tell from the Richler sendoff, which was ador-ing, prolonged, and occasionally moving, particularly after it settled down and the family got things under control. Richler deserves to be a Canadian cultural icon, and his many influential friends are doing what's needed to secure that. But at the outset there were some distinctly off-key notes amid the eulogies. In part this was a matter of too many people puffing Richler as a brilliant, uncompro-mising man who didn't suffer fools at all, let alone gladly. Since this was probably the best-publicized facet of Richler's public persona, it was hardly revelatory.

There were also a few more-than-flagrant self-betrayals among the eulogizers: Sondra Gotlieb's down-the-end-of-her-nose infer-ence that her table manners and dinner-party invitations were better than Richler's; Peter Gzowski's commemoration — written in the cloying Morningside-caller-from-North-Bay dialect — had little to impart beyond implying that Richler had always been interested in whatever obsessed Gzowski himself (which I doubt), and that the two were great, great pals, no one closer (which I'm sure was the case, because Richler, for all his prickliness, was a deeply sociable man); scrunchy-faced Newfoundlander Rex Murphy eulogized Richler in Conrad Black's prose style, drowning whatever point he wanted to make in rhetoric so foppish it would require several hours of decoding to extract and decontaminate. Others, mostly in the electronic media, talked lugubriously and solemnly about Richler's honesty, his backhanded yet somehow forthright and undeniable patriotism — and about how he couldn't possibly have included them among the barge-loads of media fools he skewered so effort-lessly one got the impression he could have done it in his sleep. Silly stuff all, prattling in the face of the Grim Reaper, which was something Richler himself never indulged in.

I don't mean to sound cynical about Richler, because I'm not. However lame and self-serving some of these platitude-laden eulogies got, the outpouring of affection for Richler was profoundly moving and didn't really falsify his accomplishments. The accumulated effect had me, for one, admiring Richler more than I already did. But it also made me take a more careful measure of the man, who I'd come to think of as an aspect of our cultural weather I was free to ignore.

Mordecai Richler and I were not friends, or even friendly. I was in the same room with him perhaps a dozen times, but the only occasion on which we spoke to one another was in Saskatoon in 1990, at a well-intentioned but badly thought-out conference on the subject of humour. One of the very bad ideas this conference had was to put the two of us on a panel with several completely crazed female stand-up comedians to talk about what it is that makes people laugh and why laughing is important. Putting Richler and me together was merely lousy programming, but one of the female comedians on the panel was so distraught at being asked to be serious and think through some ideas in public together with a couple of older men that there was a tangible threat she would either commit suicide on the spot or try to stab Richler and/or me to death. Richler responded to this, and to the several other potential indignities of the situation, by showing contempt for both audience and occasion. I didn't think the audience, which in Saskatchewan is as likely to include dry-cleaning-plant operators from North Battleford as the professional art thugs and airheads who show up for these events elsewhere in the country, deserved any contempt. I said as much, and Richler and I glowered at each other in front of the audience until the saner of the comedians dithered her way to a subject matter she was convinced was acceptably about her.

Despite the incident, I've regarded Richler with the good will one writer accords another who is older and more accomplished. In addition, I am friendly with Richler's eldest son, Daniel, and very much like and admire his literary and television work. I've also met younger sons Noah and Jake socially. They're less sanguine beings than Daniel, but both are intellectually capable and articulate. A reprint of Jake's mid-90s *GQ* article about his father that appeared in the *National Post* was arguably the most insightful piece that appeared after his death. Mordecai Richler wasn't only a good novelist. He was good at parenting.

I have three things to add to what I've read and heard since his death. One has to do with Richler's place in Canadian cultural and political history, and the second involves a more accurate definition of the "honesty" that the electronic media has ascribed to him. The third is a private insight about parenting and novel-writing that Richler's passing has precipitated.

Mordecai Richler's fame amongst members of the Canadian media, and his standing amongst the nation's political and cultural elites, are largely the product of his humiliation of Quebec's separatist government at the exact moment its cachet was peaking. Richler's 1991 *New Yorker* article, "Inside/Outside," made an international laughing stock of Quebec's language laws, which were a philosophically less serious but politically more sexy issue than the xenophobia and anti-Semitism Richler understood were still lurking within francophone Quebec society. The *New Yorker* article — which was shortly afterward elaborated into a book — made Quebec and its separatist government look particularly foolish in America, which is where, in the minds of Québecoises, looking good most matters. And once Richler got the knife between the ribs of the separatists, he twisted it relentlessly and accurately — so much so that after the Quebec referendum there was a substantial transfer of hostility amongst separatist Québecoises from English Canada to him. It might be the case that enough hostility shifted that it diffused the energies that could have led to another quick referendum. Certainly Richler provided a more swift-witted opposition to Québecois xenophobia than the collection of Jean Chretien and his bumbling federalists have mustered.

In that sense, English Canada may owe Mordecai Richler an even greater debt of gratitude than the one it has acknowledged. But there is a dark side to this. Had the 1995 referendum vote slipped another percentage point or so to the separatists, the same political commentators who were snuggling up to Richler's memory would have been reviling him as the man who broke up Canada. And they wouldn't be completely wrong.

Richler was living proof that the best Canadians are not our cliché-slinging patriots or our humourless and over-earnest nationalists. He didn't write "Inside/Outside" to save Canada. His deepest concern was the anti-Semitism he detected in Quebec's language laws and in the larger political ambitions of the separatists. After that, I suspect he was more concerned about being annoyed and harassed by officious bureaucrats and other Anglophobic fools in Quebec than saving Canada. It's no accident that Richler parted political company with Mel Hurtig in what was a Canadian nationalist version of the Hemingway-Gertrude Stein parting — with Richler playing Gertrude Stein.

My second point is about Richler's "honesty." Honesty was never among Richler's primary virtues or faults, as it can't be for any worthwhile writer, whether he or she is producing fiction or not. I'm not suggesting that Richler wasn't direct and truthful, which he often was when a deserving target appeared in his sights. I'm merely pointing out that honesty can't, by definition, be exercised in politics, and its presence within cultural and personal matters is generally accompanied by excessive volumes of self-aggrandizing sincerity, which is among the most subtly violent forms of human stupidity. The more grainy truth about Mordecai Richler was that from early in his career he was coldly assiduous in his presentation of himself and his artistic and geo-ethnic concerns. He self-mythologized himself and Montreal's St. Urbain Street more successfully than any writer in Canadian history has presented her or his cultural merchandise. He did this because he thought that it would get him the audience he needed, and he was right. He was consistent about this, and he was focused, which are qualities normally associated with honesty only where accompanied by excessive grinning. Mordecai Richler wasn't famous for grinning.

What some of the very simple-minded eulogizers were lauding as

Richler's honesty was in fact a profound and possibly unique (to Canada) cultural and artistic courage. Richler was, as a man and as an artist, completely unafraid to piss people off if he thought it mattered. Admittedly, there was also a part of him that liked to piss people off for the sheer fun of it. But even then, he doesn't seem to have let such private pleasures interfere with his pursuit of issues he thought were important. When it counted, he showed up with whatever weapon would have the greatest effect, and here, as elsewhere, his instincts were usually accurate: needle, boning knife, bludgeon. Whichever he employed, he also came with his facts straight and his research done. He never arrived armed only with sincerity or honesty. He was marvellously without such fatuousness.

My last point has to do with Richler's parenting skills and with the way he was able to exercise them. I'd have thought Mordecai Richler would, by the testimony of his children alone, be remembered as a loving but unorthodox parent who made his children stronger and more articulate than they might have been — all without alienating them. With thirty-two- and twenty-three-year-old sons of my own, I have a vivid sense of how difficult a job it is to raise children to capable adulthood without convincing them along the way that you're either an incompetent boob or an authoritarian asshole — or both. But my friend Phinjo Gombu, whose own daughter is three years younger than my five-year-old, made a remark shortly after Richler's death that made me see something I'd missed.

When he's working evenings at his newspaper job, Phinjo often shows up at Dooney's Café before nine in the morning with his daughter. His wife has gone back to work, and they're sharing childcare between them. Phinjo does mornings when he's working nights, and nights when he's working days. The Monday after Richler's death, Phinjo blew into Dooney's with his daughter just after I'd arrived from dropping my daughter off at her summer play-school. When I mentioned the subject that had been everywhere in the weekend papers, he remarked that Richler was the last of the old-time novelists. I asked what he meant, but his daughter was fussing, and instead of settling down to explain himself, he had to walk her around the streets in the stroller until she fell asleep. He returned twenty minutes later, parked the sleeping daughter and stroller a few tables away, and sat down.

His datum, it turned out, was Jake Richler's reprinted *GQ* piece, which he saw as proof that Richler the elder had been a chauvinist parent. I agreed, but suggested that focusing on his life that way was undeservedly harsh. Richler, I said, had hardly been a remote parent — at least he was there, and the excellent mental health of his kids is the ultimate test of parenting effect. But as we talked, it became clear that rather than lodging a complaint, Phinjo was making an observation about the way things were done by Richler's generation. The women raised the kids, the husbands did the money-making. From that, Phinjo was merely connecting the dots in a rather thoughtful way. We agreed that the divisions of labour Richler enjoyed in his household were necessary to getting big novels written, or at least that without them the work would have been weaker, and the novels almost certainly fewer and shorter in length. That, it turned out, was what Phinjo meant by "last of the old-time novelists." "You and I couldn't accept that kind of situation even if it was offered to us," he said.

I agreed, adding that Richler's domestic situation simply isn't being offered anymore. The moment I said it, I realized that neither of us resented the changes we've seen between Richler's generation and ours. It is, simply, the way things are now, and the compensatory bonuses we get are adequate. But it does mean that anyone writing a novel today has to be one or more of several things Richler wasn't: wealthy enough to have full-time servants to take care of domestic life, socially and interpersonally reclusive, elderly, gay, or childless. As a writer, Richler did not have to attend to child-rearing or other time-consuming domestic chores. Today, domestically committed middle-class heterosexuals — male or female — have to find other ways to write, and other, briefer forms to work in, because the kinds of concentration accorded novelists of Richler's generation simply aren't possible. There will be no more *Barney's Version*s written by heterosexual novelists with families.

I'm not sure losing novels created by heterosexual male novelists with full domestic lives is in and of itself a tragic loss. One could argue, as I have elsewhere, that the novel is a senile form and ripe for transformation. Removing so huge a demographic from its production zone will likely speed up the process. That said, the quality and depth of Mordecai Richler's characterizations indicate that the loss will be substantial, and that we'll miss him on that count, too.

How I Got a New American Education

I HAVE A NEW AMERICAN EDUCATION even though I've been a Canadian nationalist most of my adult life. That isn't quite the same as being educated American and thus having, as some of the nuttier Canadian cultural nationalists like Robin Mathews think, the same beliefs as George W. Bush or whoever the American villain-of-the-month is. It means that I was educated by Americans who were developing a set of ideas that originated (mostly) in the United States. It also means that I think that writing is meant to have an effect in the world, and that it is most interesting when committed in the name of values that are politically cosmopolitan rather than national or aesthetic. Such writing can, but is not consciously designed to, merely contribute to national identity.

There's nothing very grand here, and nothing to threaten the integrity of Canadian culture. But let me explain it anyway. The early years of my writing life are hard to distinguish from a very modestly produced and circulated Vancouver literary magazine called *Iron* that ran some twenty issues between 1966 and 1978. The magazine came out of then newly opened Simon Fraser University and was the production — and workspace — of a group of students who were primarily influenced by the New American Poetry, the literary movement identified by the publication of Donald M. Allen's 1960 anthology of the same name.

Allen's anthology offered a selection of American poets working in the roughly defined intellectual and formal line forged by Ezra Pound and William Carlos Williams. Its concept of poetics argued for a verse line and diction dictated by the individual's ability to think, compose, and speak it in normal speech idiom. The New American poets wrote without disguising or undermining the particularities of their private and public identities, which were treated as one and the same. The leading poets of the New American Poetry — from our point of view — were Charles Olson, Robert Duncan, Jack Spicer, Robert Creeley, Edward Dorn, Denise Levertov, Allen Ginsberg, Gary Snyder, and Frank O'Hara, in roughly that order of importance.

Because *Iron* came out of the West Coast of Canada, it was relatively free of the self-conscious cultural nationalism then prevalent in the rest of the country. Most of the young writers involved were students of American-born and -educated Robin Blaser, who had accepted a faculty post at Simon Fraser in 1966. The magazine thus tended to move, whenever it could escape the overbearing influence of Charles Olson, to the poetry and Orphic images of Robert Duncan, Blaser's fellow San Franciscan. That swiftly brought us to the then recently deceased but intellectually rowdy and more accessible Jack Spicer, and to Blaser himself, who was very much alive. Blaser was expanding his concerns beyond the limits of his mentors and peers at that point in his career, at least in the quality and range of his intellectual interests. In a sense, coming to Vancouver allowed him to reinvent himself, and the energy released was available to anyone willing to hook on.

Olson's approach to literary composition, at least during the early years of his career, had been to politicize the processes involved, a dysorthodoxy which moved to make poetic speech historical and public testimony rather than the lyrical expression of a private cosmology — or cosmetology, as it seemed to us at the time — that then characterized nearly all poetry. Duncan's approach was to inject a powerful homoerotic charge into the mechanics of composition, without really challenging Olson's politicization. The two streams provided us with an attractive balance, particularly with Blaser's gentle pedagogy, which for its considerable rigour, wasn't dogmatic. If you weren't stupid and were willing to work, you were free to study whatever you liked.

The principal startup people in *Iron* (not all of whom published work in it) were, in reverse alphabetical order, the painter Renee Van Halm, Sharon Thesen, Jim Taylor, Henk and Tanya Suijs, Colin Stuart, Ken Lindemere (who later named his North Vancouver music store "Iron Music"), Neap Hoover, Alban Goulden, and me. Others who became involved over the next several years included Victoria Walker, Karl Siegler, Stan Persky, Tom McGauley, Gladys Hindmarch, Brett Enemark, Michael Boughn, and Cliff Andstein, who later went on to head the B.C. Federation of Labour, but was then studying economics and wondering if he really didn't prefer photography. I edited most of the first fifteen issues of the magazine, while Brett Enemark edited the last four or five. Along the way we got generous infusions of energy and no little amount of production money from Ralph Maud, a Welsh-American who had been hired by SFU to a full professorship as a Dylan Thomas scholar, but arrived in Vancouver a Charles Olson acolyte who was reluctant to discuss Thomas unless under duress.

There were other professorial influences on us beyond those of Blaser and Maud, of course. We were also influenced — mostly negatively — by the horde of tight-assed academic clerks hired when North America's universities expanded during the 1960s. These clerks have now taught several generations of students that literature is a strata of quaintly obtuse and obscure arrangements of language written by unruly individuals in need of supervision, whose work requires expert amplification and reorganization. Many of the clerks hired by SFU were Americans who couldn't believe their good fortune at finding themselves on a track to achieve early tenure while they weren't much older than their students. Few were intellectuals, and fewer still had scholarly aspirations. They wanted well-paid jobs that didn't require any physical labour or arduous thought, and that's what they made them into. They busied themselves with self-serving faculty association matters that secured their jobs, fattened their pensions, and altered the curriculum to accommodate whatever intellectual nitwittery was fashionable and easy to teach. In the classroom, they did what they could to professionalize — or simply undermine — our interest in literature.

Fortunately, the professors weren't all mediocre clerks. Along with Ralph Maud there was the quixotic Leonard Minsky, who taught some of us to speak Middle English with a Brooklyn accent (and others of us how hazardous posing as a Marxist revolutionary could be to an academic career if one didn't have tenure). Perhaps the most sanguine influence was that of the late Rob Dunham, who taught some of us to respect the Romantic poets, even William Wordsworth. Like Maud and Blaser, these men were Americans. George Bowering, a fine poet in his own right, joined the English department at SFU around 1970, but we regarded him as a contemporary, and thus were quite willing to play baseball with him but not take his courses or treat him very seriously as a teacher of poetics.

Iron appeared irregularly and in changing formats. The irregularity was largely a product of the laziness of its editorial board and, to a lesser extent, of the general shift in gender privileges that was occurring at the time. In 1966, educated women contributed to the general hubbub primarily while typing manuscripts and stencils, but they were beginning to notice that being as talented and intelligent as the men around them entitled them to an equal degree of arrogance and lack of industry. The result was a lot of bickering over work assignments, and one or two young men learning to touchtype. The format changes in *Iron* were partly dictated by this, but an equal influence was print technology improvements: mimeography to offset to high-speed xerography. The last issue of the first series was printed on a Xerox 9200, the first of the now-ubiquitous high-speed photocopy machines that have replaced offset print and other liquid ink technologies.

There was another dynamic contributing to *Iron*'s inertia and production chaos. By the early 1970s, most of the writers involved in *Iron* had either left the university or were in graduate school, which is to say they now believed that the physical work of putting out literary magazines ought to be done by undergraduates or other underlings, even though it was difficult to find anyone willing to play second fiddle to a bunch of scruffy poets with no money. We were moving on, in other words, if not exactly up.

Because *Iron* evolved along with the young writers who were producing it — very rapidly and with no guarantee of improvement — there was no "typical" issue of the magazine. But the twelfth issue, appearing in 1971 under the title "Serious Iron," accurately encapsulates most of the magazine's characteristics and preoccupations, including its not-always-charming inattention to fine detail. "Serious Iron" isn't sequenced with earlier or later issues, nor is it dated except for an October 1971 notation on the editorial page, which identifies the editor as "Linda Parker." Ms. Parker was a young Massachusetts visual artist who was close to Charles Olson during his last years. She'd written a postcard to Brett Enemark, criticizing the chumminess she'd detected in an earlier issue of *Iron* and suggesting that the frivolous practice of dedicating poems to one another was making *Iron* both hard for outsiders to penetrate and more than a little ungracious.

Ms. Parker was right about most of this, which quite naturally infuriated us. The form "Serious Iron" took was a counterattack on Ms. Parker's view of poetry — and of us. On the cover is a photograph of Tom McGauley, Sharon Thesen, Alban Goulden, Brett Enemark, and me gazing solemnly at the camera, dressed in what we imagined was a parody of polite writerly garb. Books are piled on the table, and the only things that give us away as not, respectively, Robert Lowell, Marianne Moore, Richard Wilbur, Karl Shapiro, and W.S. Merwin are the other details in the photo. There was a cheap plastic lamp with a dime-store Tiffany cupola shade in the middle of the table, a clamp-lamp shining directly at the camera with a cord running diagonally to a window, and a map of north-central British Columbia *circa* 1818 — stolen from the SFU library's copy of Daniel William Harmon's *Diaries* — tacked to the wall. That was our approximation of history and high culture.

The biographical notes at the end of the fifty-page issue were a run-on gag testifying to the extreme personal and professional seriousness of everyone appearing in the issue, and the editorial page that followed, purportedly written by Parker herself, has her saying: "Seriously, I think Vancouver ought to smarten up, inject some gravity into the form of its magazines, and perhaps take a bath now and again. *The Paris Review* is a good magazine to emulate, it's always objective and judicious and we all know that leads in the right direction. Don't we?" The "editor" goes on in a similarly heavy-handed way to deny that Shelley, Byron, and Keats spent time together in Italy, and hacks at some poor poet named Frederick Bock for publishing two poems in issue VII-3 of the *Quarterly Review of Literature* that "had utterly no effect on anyone," blaming the "fiercely objective editors" of *QRL* for arranging the issue to ensure the non-effect.

Overkill? Sure. Did the chumminess of our small community exclude others? Yes, certainly — Patrick Lane carps about it to this day. But the exclusivity had little to do with any of us thinking we were superior poets, or superior beings. We'd created *Iron* from realistic motives and with modest expectations. We didn't bother to make these visible to others because we thought they were self-evident.

The modesty came about in an interesting way. Shortly after I reached university, I asked composer, Ezra Pound scholar, and musical educator R. Murray Schafer, then pioneering the university's communications department, what he thought were the best ways to learn my craft and get my writing into print. I admired Schafer because he'd been making a career out of witty insolence in the face of authority, and his answer was characteristically unconventional — and useful.

"When you're starting off," he told me, "you learn best from your peers, people you can argue things out with in person, people your own age. So go off and make your own magazine. Use it to publish your own work while you're learning your craft. Don't send out your poems so strangers can judge how closely they resemble the ones they're writing. And never mind trying to impress the big shots. They're old, they're tired, and they'll always like you best while you're on their farm team. When your work is good enough, the people who will get it before a bigger audience will come looking for you."

"The best thing about being a student," he'd concluded, "is that you get to *be* a student. Don't let anyone cheat you out of that experience."

A few weeks later, we started *Iron*, more or less directly on the basis of Schafer's advice. I'd like to pretend that the choice of "Iron" for our magazine's name reflected our understanding of the importance of irony in art, but that would be a lie. The magazine was so named because iron isn't gold or lead, and it isn't refined enough to be called steel. Iron was simply a material among the basic raw materials of human improvement, which is what we believed poetry was. *Iron* — the magazine — didn't claim to be anything at all except basic student inquiry, along with a healthy dose of insolence. In an era when the literary magazines that weren't undertaking to represent vastly more than was reasonable (*West Coast Review, Contemporary Literature*) were trying to steal their names and their energy from cultures — mostly Native Indian — that would have found the appropriations exploitive, puerile, or sentimental, that modesty of intention would remain a defining virtue.

In 1971 I thought "Serious Iron" was extremely witty, and I carried that recollection across the intervening years as *Iron*'s best issue without really asking myself why it was so. It wasn't until I looked through a photocopy of the issue thirty years later that I realized I didn't recall a single piece of writing in it. As I read through the different pieces, it became clear to me that I was reading some of them for the first time, even though I'd edited the issue. What strikes me, as a close-to-disinterested reader in the twenty-first century, is the disjunction between the individual pieces of writing and the general attitude of the magazine itself. The poems and essays in "Serious Iron" are paraclete to the point of sycophancy, serious to the point of weepy earnestness, and rhinestoned with the cosmological sentimentality and bombast that characterized Charles Olson's late work. By contrast, the magazine is ironic, playful, and disrespectful of authority, including that of Olson himself.

At least part of the reason for the disjunction between the magazine and its contents had to do with the geographical and cultural origins of those involved in it. Most of the young writers active in starting *Iron* were from small towns in Western Canada — Sharon Thesen, Brett Enemark, and I were from Prince George, B.C.; Neap Hoover was from Vernon, B.C.; Gladys Hindmarch from Ladysmith on Vancouver Island; and Alban Goulden from Medicine Hat, Alberta. We were awed, in our different ways, by contact with what seemed to us "real" writers, and honestly attracted to the ragged-edged vernacular of the New American Poetry, which was much more local to us than the stilted diction of the contemporary Canadian poetry we could find to read. The New American Poetry was also better tuned to our hormone-driven preoccupations than the sterile aesthetic records of emotional attrition, lip-bitten incapacity, and mendacious silences that had filled academic lyric poetry for decades during and after the Second World War, both in Canada and elsewhere. We wanted to write poetry, sure, but we weren't prepared to be tea-sipping aesthetes in a world of miniature aesthetic jewellery boxes.

The heterosexual writers in *Iron* were drawn to Olson — I was perhaps foremost among them — because Olson was so *frantically* heterosexual, and thus, at root, full of the heterodox confusions that Spicer/Blaser/Duncan simply didn't evince. No one had bothered to tell us, you see, that poetry has historically been the one branch of human experience and enterprise within which one is able to openly search for oneself and for one's gender likeness. It is in the nature of the Orphic to be uniquely open to the homogeneous, and to homosexuality, the latter of which had then just barely begun to be freed from its camouflaging codes. For the most part we didn't know those codings were there, and tended to dismiss them when we discovered them.

It is also possible that we were immunized to some degree — against the homo/Orphic bias, against our teachers' intellectual shortcomings, and against the early New Age excesses of the New American Poetry — by having grown up in small towns. That experience equipped those who survived it with an innate skepticism about how reliable people with authority are. We weren't quite at the point reached by a later generation of Western Canadian poets, who don't trust anyone who hasn't lost a limb in an industrial accident, but we understood that sort of concern.

That skepticism got us, at least, to a point where we were able to critique the mostly phony and self-aggrandizing enterprise of literary magazine writing and the publishing of verse. I think that skepticism also enabled some of us, despite our awe, to glimpse the self-absorption and egomania of Olson and Duncan. Though we were under their influence, we tried to deflate our small corner of it to dimensions manageable enough that we could imagine ourselves taking an active part. If our mentor Blaser found this insolence troubling, he never let it show, except to make it very clear to us that Jack Spicer would have approved. When it came to doing our own writing, we were on our own, but Schafer's advice — along with Blaser's teaching — made us understand that it would be a long, uphill grind and that we'd better do what we could to amuse ourselves along the way.

The different pieces of writing that appear in "Serious Iron" are distractingly full of typographical errors (even substituting "peom" for "poem" at one point), and most are infused with silly astrological and tarot card references and a now-mortifying fan club mentality about Charles Olson. The opening piece, for instance, is a series of notes Ralph Maud wrote after visiting Olson in Gloucester a year or so before he died of liver cancer in 1970. Thirty years later I can just barely penetrate Maud's expressives, and then only because I was involved in transcribing the lecture Olson gave when he visited Vancouver in 1965 that was eventually published under Maud's editorship as *Causal Mythology*. On their merits, Maud's notes didn't deserve the lead spot in the magazine, but, whoops, I recall that Maud had pretty much financed that particular issue by arranging for it to be printed in the university's print room.

More or less accidentally, Maud's shorthand memoir also documents the strain of American cultural arrogance that was present in those years. Most of the Americans we were close to, like Blaser and Stan Persky, quickly acclimatized to Canada and have since been more conscientious citizens than the vast majority of those of us who are native-born. But in 1970 the discourse around Charles Olson was astonishing for its Pax Americana, and it is that impression, not Maud's reverence for Olson, that articulates most clearly today.

"Serious Iron" proceeds with excerpts from Gladys (now Maria) Hindmarch's account of her first and only pregnancy, and that is followed by Tom McGauley's transcription of a July 1971 lecture by British poet and editor Jeremy Prynne on Olson's *Maximus IV, V, & VI*, which Prynne edited for British publisher Jonathan Cape in 1968. The issue wandered from there into some very good poems by Victoria Walker, an extremely personal and ambiguous one by me, and some equally obscure self-declarations by others. It ends with an old Robert Creeley essay we republished under the (imaginary) Havana Copyright Conventions, which made any intellectual materials the property of whoever wanted to read them. None of the pieces warrant comment here except the transcript of Prynne's lecture.

In giving Prynne's transcribed lecture a prominent place in the issue, we were allowing an editor to review his own book, but no one seemed to think that was odd. In our minds, Olson was always as much an embattled and underappreciated "cause" as a literary figure. We weren't the only ones who saw him that way, either. Prynne's defence of Olson's new book, which nearly everyone was finding to be a mixture of incomprehensible mythographic ravings interspersed with the same kind of fragmentary lyricisms that mark Pound's last Cantos, was that it was "noble, simple," and not confessional or lyric.

"We participate," Prynne says, in an elliptical rhetoric worthy of Olson himself, "in the condition of being. And the condition of being is thankfully beyond the condition of meaning. Oh yes, the whole language has that vibrancy, that steady vibrancy of the singular curvature which is equivalent to what was anciently called nobility."

Parse those three sentences if you can. I couldn't at the time, and today it most resembles the verbal preening of a male peacock trying to balance on the top of a very tall statue and display his tail feathers at the same time. But in 1971 I understood the *expressive* content of Prynne's self-review, and I still do. Prynne gave his lecture, remember, not quite a year after Olson's death, an event that by itself prevented anyone in his extended community from making a fair-minded evaluation of his later work — Prynne included, who was as detectably in awe of the Great Man as anyone in the audience for that lecture.

Today, it seems to me that Olson's later work is much diminished in skill and coherence compared to his early poetry and hard to defend in other than expressive terms. The condition of being, in other words, bloody well shouldn't exist beyond the condition of meaning. In his early poems, Olson had been a civic-minded writer grounded in a detail-driven appreciation for local historical, biological, and political conditions. He'd used those public contents, and the enhancement of private context they'd provided, to work his way beyond the Pound/Williams-inspired dislike for the limitations of existing poetic forms of expression and perhaps for artifice itself, to ones that seemed more accurately democratic and liberating. Olson's was a laudable undertaking, but it ran aground on the same currents that had provided its essential energy: the growing cultural ascendance of figure over ground, and the various self-determination and self-discovery and exhibition movements that grew parallel with it.

Sometime in the early 1960s, Olson became, without anyone noting it, obsessed with imposing a capriciously self-involved and possibly clinically manic-depressive "cosmology" on everything and anyone that came within his range. His poetry moved from the assignable declarativeness that had made it so accessible, to a celebratory mode that was alternately soaring in its lyricism and hectoringly pedantic about whatever obscure piece of scholarship he happened to be shaking between his teeth. Most damning, the poems he produced under these conditions of composition are pretty well impenetrable unless one believes, a priori, in their coherence. For Olson, language became indistinguishable from self, which, with the Language poets who followed a decade later, he didn't distinguish from identity.

Now, the young *Iron* poets were also deeply suspicious of purely confessional lyric poetry. To us it seemed boring and laughably solipsistic. That instinct, born of the incipient nuclear Armageddon that had threatened to rain down on us throughout our childhood and adolescence, told us that our poetic — and other — concerns ought to be cosmopolitan, easy to understand, and as swift as the world had become. From there we were easily convinced by Olson's early works of the importance of localism and specificity because it meant that our perceptions of reality, even in our non-New York or San Francisco part of the world, were as authentic as those of anyone else.

The claim that Olson — and later his followers — made, that a balancing of particularism and cosmology constituted the compositional conditions for epic, was also seductive, even if the registration pins didn't exactly line up. We'd grown up with the daily threat of nuclear extinction, so an involvement in something grander than a lot of sucky-faced self-therapy seemed like our birthright — or at least a way of taking control over some small corner of it. But the scattering of Olson's intelligence that occurs with and after *Maximus IV, V, & VI* left me scrambling for perspective, even at the time. I kept thinking that cosmology and epic ought to be more than a matter of flamboyantly filtering subjective experiences with the moon through the tarot pack or the Greek earth goddesses. But since it didn't seem so to anyone else, what did I know?

In hindsight I see that Olson's late work — I remain convinced of the value of his early ideas, and the poetry they produced — was epic only because Olson was himself physically epic in dimension: a very large, strange man with an overwhelming vitality and a hurricane ego. "I am Charles Olson: a Cosmos" was the declarative theme that emerged everywhere from this second, expansive version of the Maximus Poems. As small-town kids living in a non-imperial country, we instinctively traced this back to Walt Whitman's Pax Americana egomania, which we found funny enough that we often parodied the famous phrase using thick German accents: "*Ich bin Valt Vitman, ein Cosmos . . . ,*" and then clicking our heels as we gave the Nazi salute.

No doubt we should have been making fun of Olson's bombastic excesses too, and in our confused way that's what the framing of "Serious Iron" was trying to do. But we were also "under the influence" of Olson's mystique, and of the people who had been flattened to intellectual two-dimensionality by personal contact with this Large, Great Man and his Large, Great, less-than-coherent Epic.

I had inklings that there was something amiss in Olson's way of confiding in us as if we were all Americans. As a Canadian and as a northerner I did not naturally share his New England Yankee sense of being among the Elect. Where I'd come from, to be chosen was to be singled out, usually for a thumping. My instincts were more attuned to keeping still and hoping the bullies didn't beat the shit out of me for being lippy and different. But my raised hackles over that were, as it were, mere shivers of irritation, less compelling than the general hormonal rage of being a male in my twenties, which was making me mistake the loneliness of adult life for cosmology, and vice versa. Olson, in his madness, fed that rage in ways few other poets of the era could have.

Thirty years later, some of Olson's work — the early essays and the civic and locally grounded poems of *Maximus I–XXII* — remain a part of my imagination of the world. But while fragments of the later work achieve a muscular sort of lyricism, too much of it was fragmentary incoherence, and some of it was plain bombast and bullshit. The absurd intellectual orthodoxy Olson inspired at the time so obscured this that it was almost a full decade before I was able to admit to myself that I had understood very little of *Maximus IV, V, & VI*, and virtually nothing at all of the posthumously published *The Maximus Poems Volume Three*. I'd merely agreed to pretend I did for social reasons. And so, I've since found, did a lot of people I like and respect.

Olson did show us how to write and think with a respect for particularity and without fear of abstraction. That was good. But along with overestimating the cultural importance of verse, he offered no useful clues about structure and the weighting between the local and the structural. The *Zeitgeist* of the era, which was much more interested in liberating the individual from the past than in giving anyone a balanced education, offered no directions either.

Yet having said that, I still believe that it *was* better to think cosmologically than globally (as the latter has devolved), and better to think locally than to measure value in terms of nations and the myriad other human exclusions that now make up our politics. To have been foolishly partisan to a noble attempt to make the world larger and more unified through the powers of language was a better project than to be afflicted in the way we are today, forced to articulate our understandings through our individual complexes of ethnicity and preference, and through the phobias that ethnicities don't seem able to exist without. There was less hate then, particularly amongst liberal-minded people, which is what scholars and poets and students ought to be. Today, liberals are compelled to hate one another almost as virulently as people hated in the 1930s. Today, educated people hate rapists, racists, monetarists, male supremacists, ableists, even environmentalists, all the while wondering what it is in themselves that has become so hateful. Today's intellectual and artistic climates make me, for one, long for some epic, or at least for some of the cosmology that in Olson made the world feel large and welcoming.

I suppose it is possible — just barely — to regard the *contents* of "Serious Iron" as our attempt to mourn Olson's passing, our way to rue the depressing truth that the Great Big Father had gone off into the aether and left us to ponder his imponderables with no one to guide us but some thoroughly mortal professor-clerks and a few older poets roughly our own size. I was happy to have Blaser and other men and women of more mortal dimensions to work with, and under. In Blaser, I still think we got the best teacher who came out of the New American Poetry, one whose later work has proved at least the equal in quality to that of the major figures. Blaser not only survived, he grew.

I'm not sure, anymore, exactly what Olson and Duncan and Blaser and even the professor-clerks, good or mediocre, thought they were teaching us to do and be in the late 1960s. But I'm increasingly aware that what we were learning from them, willy-nilly, was tolerance. Maybe tolerance was something that was in the air we breathed in those days. However it was delivered, my generation of writers learned it well enough that we have since practised tolerance at a level of skill and depth not approached before or since in human history. Unfortunately, tolerance is, as intellectual and life-projects go, both limited and flawed. It much too easily disintegrates into moral cowardice, indifference, and silence, and the backlash it has precipitated amongst younger intellectuals is worrisome because it has undermined their respect for thought itself.

On the other hand, Olson, Blaser, and the New American Poetry got some of us to question the liberal and anthropocentric humanism we'd been brought up with. Questioning the humanist enterprise was always a *primary* element of Blaser's pedagogy, and it is one for which I am deeply grateful. I can still recall the heart-stopping moral conundrum Blaser created for me when he suggested that individual survival might not be the highest good. If nothing else, that alerted me, permanently, that humanism deserves closer and more critical scrutiny than it has gotten. It received little more than lip-service for the first fifty years of the twentieth century, and a badly thought-through turning against it by environmentalists and anti-racists has been the clandestine fuel for a bizarre outbreak of species-wide self-loathing in the twenty-five years leading up to the millennium.

As for *Iron*, its biggest virtue, in retrospect, was that it didn't out-live its usefulness. It helped a group of young writers educate them-selves, and then it died, permitting those involved with it to move on. There are no great undiscovered aesthetic artifacts to be found in its pages, no precocious but hidden John Keats, despite the presence of several young poets who aspired to the role. That is all as it should be. We were, in the end, students learning a craft that, because it requires one to know the culture itself in its now-immense complex-ity and breadth, takes several decades to master.

In that respect, the best qualities of *Iron* and of the group of writ-ers who were my contemporaries and cross-pollinators were those that were visible on the surface of "Serious Iron": insolence, skepticism struggling with the wish for a larger world, a blossoming sense of irony that did not descend into cynicism, and a willingness to make fun in a world that gave credibility only to making abstract love and preparing for and making war. In the ultimate sense, the education it provided was cosmopolitan, not new or American at all. It was the blueprint for the self-involved cosmopolitanism my generation has practised when it is at its best.

The Anthology

ON A STEAMY AFTERNOON on Toronto's Bloor Street last summer, I happened to glance inside a cardboard box abandoned beside a parking meter. It being Canada and not Northern Ireland or the West Bank, the box didn't explode in my face. It contained books.

Because I'm too middle class to be dumpster-diving other people's intellectual rejectamenta, I meant only to glance into the box and pass by. But one of the books caught my eye — specifically, the Northwest Coast Indian symbol on its cover. For sure it wasn't the book's uninformative title, in bold print just above the graphic: *New West Coast*. I reached inside and rescued the book, sneering a little at the pun in the title and at the cutesy cultural appropriation of the graphic, an abstraction of two bears, bookended.

That was when I noticed the smaller, lower-case, red-print subtitle — *72 contemporary british columbia poets* — and the editor's name, writ smaller still. It was my seventeenth-century-literature professor from Simon Fraser University, a nice man named Fred Candelaria who composed music for classical guitar and wrote poems that sometimes sounded a little like Emily Dickinson with a winkle, but more often imitated living poets he thought could help his poetry career. Candelaria edited the official university literary magazine and sent out his poems with a covering letter using the magazine's letterhead — a clear signal that if you published him, he'd publish you. I caught myself wondering cynically why he'd chosen so few of the poets in B.C., of which there are enough to make seventy-two anthologies with seventy-two poets each. But a less cynical curiosity soon gripped me. Geez, what percentage of the self-expression-crazed idiots who'd exposed their innermost thoughts to the clamouring public did I know?

I checked the title page for the date of publication. It was a 1977 production out of Intermedia Press, one of many long-gone, little-mourned literary presses of the era. Then I checked the table of contents. About half of the poets listed were familiar to me, and half of those still active. Life being what it was on the West Coast when I lived there, I was able to count ten I'd played baseball with or against at one time or another. And as I scanned the list a second time, I got an unexpected shock. My name was in the table of contents.

That's when I recalled the special feature of this anthology. Along with exposing their innermost sensitivities in their poems, the authors had been invited to explain why they'd exposed themselves. Another detail drifted up from the memory sump. The explanations offered had been so silly — mine included — that when I received my author copies in the mail and read my statement along with five or six of the others, the posturing and posing was so humiliating that I tossed the books into the nearest wastepaper basket and resolved to forget that it had ever been published.

I'd succeeded, but that isn't quite my point. The point I'd like to make — there are several — isn't personal. The first is that my experience with that innocuous box of unwanted consumer items would be rare outside English-speaking North America, and unthinkable fifty years ago in any culture. Outside a few mostly monastic enclaves for the aged or the strangely educated, books are now among the least-valued common commodities produced and/or consumed by North Americans. Books are remaindered regularly in real bookstores well below their manufacturing cost, become the primary contents of our fly-by-night retail surplus sector, and when that fails to find buyers, are pulped or abandoned on street corners. I'd be willing to challenge anyone to find another commodity that is treated with less respect by today's marketplace.

One can, I suppose, see this as a part of technology transformation. Certainly Kurt Vonnegut seemed to see it that way when he called print a temporary cultural phenomenon that is too inefficient to survive. Marshall McLuhan's followers like to claim that the guru foresaw the cultural eclipse of print, even though few of them have read enough of his work to be able to cite any specific passage that says this explicitly (not to mention that the phrase "explicit passage by McLuhan" is something of an oxymoron). Personally I'm not convinced that print will decline in importance much further than it has. The processing technologies will continue to change, and so will human reading habits and applications. Right now, Canada is producing too many books, often for reasons that don't make cultural or economic sense.

Book publishing and selling give us an object lesson in how evolution is a messy and not necessarily focused or efficient procedure. The evolution of book publishing is similar to that of panda bears, who grew so comfortable in China's lush bamboo forests that they lost their aggression and most of the omnivorous adaptive skills that make other subspecies of bears competent survivors. Now, as the bamboo forests of China disappear and the poachers outnumber the poachees by a ratio of about 50 million to one, the vegetarian pandas are doomed to preserves and zoos.

But books aren't the same thing as print, and while they're more vulnerable than print, they're hardly the cultural equivalent of pandas. Books remain our most permanent form of record-keeping, and when produced using the right materials they are the least vulnerable format by which individuals can separate themselves from the brain-scouring manipulations of the state and the corporations. A book is relatively small, sturdy, and portable. Once printed and bound, it can't be shut off from a remote location the way a radio or television set can. The processing software is built into most of us, has been since we were five or six years old, and it can't be subverted by alpha-wave gumbo forcing the brain to scan images that aren't really there. And because an individual book now flies beneath the radar of mass-production economics, it offers some degree of freedom from the built-in marketplace editorializations that make every other information technology untrustworthy.

A sizable percentage of books, whether we like to admit it or not, aren't written within the rational terms of the profit-focused economy. They are the byproduct of professional activity — as with Fred Candelaria's anthology, sort of — or are the result of passionate avocation. Someone knew something, or wanted to make a record of an investigation, and made the necessary economic sacrifices to see it through. At this point in human evolution, such books probably constitute no more than a small percentage of book sales and a slightly larger percentage of the total number of books published. Most are quickly lost in the onslaught of purely temporal and commercial bullshit from the self-help side of the publishing industry, the commercial fiction sector, and the production of pop cultural analysis and propaganda.

Admittedly, some of these books, like Fred Candelaria's obscure anthology of lower-case British Columbia poets, deserve to land up in cardboard boxes on street corners. But many don't, and I hope such books can survive in the substrata of human memory that truth and beauty have seemed able to create within any form of past and present oppression. Fifty years from now, it is these books that will likely constitute the only authentic record of what life was like in our era, and the only testimony to the dreams of beauty, kindness, and decency we had while the corporations were erecting Disneyworld and the End of History to keep us entertained while they fried the planet for profits.

The second point I'd like to make, much less apocalyptic in its implications, is that nothing in my opening anecdote will be shocking to contemporary literate Canadians. Finding boxes of books abandoned on a sidewalk or offered for sale at small fractions of their production cost is a very common experience. Similarly, the experience of writing and publishing books with no serious expectation that they will reach more than a handful of specialized readers is a depressing fact of life for all but a tiny percentage of Canadian writers.

Canada almost certainly publishes more unsellable books per capita and has more fly-by-night retail book surplus events and more books abandoned on street corners than any country in the world. In no small part this is because we're a prime repository for American overproduction. Americans know we read more than they do, probably believing we have nothing else to do in our chilly igloos, and ship accordingly. But we're also the only country in the world that publishes books for reasons of national security, or, at least, the only country in the world for whom cultural products (books, television, popular music, and some movies) are the *only* means of national self-defence that look beyond the foreshortening horizon of current events — now roughly coincident with quarterly profit forecasts, and hard to distinguish from them in any meaningful way.

Cultural production isn't a very efficient means of self-defence, and not just because there is always some nitwitted visual *artiste* deciding that executing his pet rat in public will garner him some publicity by shaking the shocked-and-appalled crowd from its customary coma. It is inefficient because the inherent unpredictability of the future makes insight appear permanently random, and because the industrial model that book publishing has slipped into places a bonus on two things that are contradictory: innovation and conventional behaviour.

Cultural innovation is the messiest and least tangible form of innovation human beings practise, one that makes normal folks impatient and irritable because the end product is almost always impossible to categorize and turn into merchandise until its origins are unrecognizable. Cultural innovation can begin with an untoward thought or activity; it can be an insight, a cognitive frame, all things that administer subtle nudges or not-so-subtle stabs between the ribs. Their effects almost never show up on quarterly profit statements until long after the corporations have forgotten where they came from.

Even the most conventional elements of cultural production are messy. Sometimes culture records our stupidity and our misdeeds for posterity. More often it glorifies our silliness and navel-gazing myopia — or is translatable simply as "Look at me!" Most frequently it is debris, but we can almost never, through the lens of orders-of-the-day, predict its value with certainty. Future generations will make those judgments, if we're lucky.

What should be said in defence of Canadian cultural products is that they aren't as unproductive as the Canadian armed forces, which merely march up and down and back and forth, fly $50-million airplanes into mountainsides, torture offshore civilians, fight in wars on behalf of the oil industry, and then hang the few heroic individuals it does produce — people like Romeo Dallaire — out to dry when it counts. It should also be noted, and not as a laughing matter, that our armed forces tend to be directed by ministers who can't quite remember if Canada fought at Vimy or Vichy Ridge.

Comparing culture with the armed forces will probably raise many more hackles around the country than my other points, which are more important. But along with scary, depressing particulars and their likely causes, maybe these are issues that should be argued out in public, not left to subsist as self-deprecating jokes.

Whatever silliness the culture convinces writers to imagine they're engaged in, their real job is to make and keep records. They also try — or should — to integrate facts of the past with the present, where facts are much harder to establish, if only because our public figures these days all too frequently confuse Vimy Ridge with Vichy. And if securing an antidote to their confusion (which is accurately reflective of the society at large under the atomizing stresses of television and other sorts of media overabundance) results in a few silly poetry anthologies that end up abandoned on the streets of a small, wealthy country, we should treat it as the cost of doing business and go about our less-important daily business with a sharp shiver of gratitude.

Plenitude and Globalized Culture

SEVERAL YEARS AGO, the *Globe & Mail* gave me a book to review by a man named Grant McCracken. Though McCracken hails from the West Coast, he had arrived at the Royal Ontario Museum via the University of Chicago as an anthropologist, an aficionado of popular culture whose previous book, *Big Hair*, was a trendy Downtown Toronto-style send-up of women's hair culture, and — not incidentally — made McCracken a minor darling on Toronto's corporate/culture cocktail party circuit. None of those quite made him a culture hero, but each was more or less a full-time commitment.

Plenitude, the book I was given to review, was a tastefully designed black-and-forest-green tome subtitled *Book One of Culture by Commotion*. It was self-published under the rather grandiose imprint of Periph:Fluide, which I gather means "on the edge and fluid" in French. In the several television interviews I'd seen McCracken do for the *Big Hair* volume, he had seemed a man who relished his work and, better, was capable of treating popular culture with a dose of deflating irony. Consequently, *Plenitude* was a book I was completely willing to be charmed by despite its ostentatious title and subtitle.

The *Globe*'s book editor, Martin Levin, hadn't given me much in the way of background for the book, so I phoned the ROM and left a message on McCracken's answering service asking him to unscramble several details that had me puzzled: who the publisher's owner/operators were, the meaning of the publisher's strange name, and the book's price. After a couple of days of telephone tag, I found myself chatting with McCracken.

Chat he did. He told me he was the sole and independent owner-operator of Periph:Fluide, and Hey! Never mind buying the book, why not download it free from the Internet, where it's much more *user-friendly*. He chattered on about his frustrations with conventional publishing and made some predictable cracks about how obsolete print has become. While I half-listened to this malarkey, I did some common-sense additions and concluded that he was either a fiscal imbecile or was being more than a little disingenuous about the finances. The name of the press, he explained, is a reference to traffic conditions on the Paris ring road. Translated roughly, it amounts to calling one's publishing house "Traffic Moving Smoothly on the 401." By the time we hung up, I was a little less prepared to be charmed.

About fifty pages into *Plenitude*, I was distinctly *not* charmed by McCracken or his book. It was all too plain that, along with the growing horde of similarly Toronto-based, self-aggrandizing but mainly academic techno-nincompoops, this author/auteur was chasing Marshall McLuhan's mantle and the now much-enhanced perks that come with it: guru status among the dull-witted corporate elites desperate to convince themselves that their greedy opportunisms have a deeper intellectual or spiritual order than those of a pack of feral dogs; seminar headlining at five to fifty grand a pop; a well-funded university centre for popcult studies and demographic modelling; and so on. The Culture by Commotion project, in other words, was meant to be McCracken's on-ramp to the fast lanes of upper-case Global Corporate Culture, with *Plenitude* as the first vehicle on.

The organizing premise of *Plenitude* — stop me if you've been finding this sermon openly preached in the business pages of every newspaper in North America — is that the atomization of political, social, and cultural values and enclaves we've experienced since the mid 1970s is a wholly positive development, one that is without precedent and without any downside.

The review I wrote for the *Globe* started by noting that "plenitude" is a word that generally isn't heard outside Anglican Church liturgy, then pointed to the twenty-one supporting inscriptions between the book's covers and the beginning of the text, the 129 names — most of them corporate leaders and cocktail circuit luminaries from the academic world — listed in the acknowledgement pages, and finally the 287 chatty footnotes that fouled the meagre 130 pages of essay text. From there, it was pretty easy to argue that *Plenitude* was a shameless and ill-disguised infomercial for McCracken as a popcult guru and for the marketplace as the righteous and inevitable determinant of all values, economic, cultural, or what-your-mother-is-talking-about-with-her-friends-this-week.

Yet by the time I'd completed and sent in the review — one of those seven-hundred-word jobs I luxuriated into slightly more than a thousand words (and for which I probably got myself tossed off the list of *Globe* reviewers) — I was more annoyed with myself than with McCracken or his book. I'd thumped him, but I hadn't been able to get at the issues the book raised. I'd ended up being merely cruel to a man whose main sins were his vivacious contempt for the past and an ambition that somehow managed to be half-baked and slick at the same time. Big deal. Maybe I'd let some air out of McCracken, but given all the support and propaganda available for neocapitalist entrepreneurs these days, probably not.

The truth is that I was more than a little bemused by the performance I'd witnessed. McCracken's intellectual and cultural values were so foreign to me he might as well have been from a different species. To get 129 people onto the acknowledgements page of one of my books, for instance, I'd have to be listing distant relatives and the people I've punched in bars. I don't know 129 people worth sucking up to, and I can't imagine what life would be like at so intense a level of purse-lipped interactivity.

So, without getting into the question of whether I'm just an old-fashioned crank or whether McCracken's brain has been addled by corporate crack, what exactly were these issues I couldn't get to?

The most important one has to do with the decay of discourse procedures the book revealed, and the possibility that this decay, which seems inextricably fused with the informational wealth we're experiencing, is making it impossible for people to carry on the open discussion of cultural semantics that is the foundation of all democratic institutions. More than anything else we do, these procedures keep us from burying axes in one another's skulls.

The issue was raised by the incontinent way *Plenitude* argues its ideas. This is a book that proceeds almost wholly by polemical overkill. Complexity theory, the semi-crackpot theory by which, a few years ago, tenured university professors tried to reinvent God without letting him or her have the power to interfere with their dental plans, gets tossed in as proof of *Plenitude*'s verity, together with a host of other sloppily posited data sources and conceptual grids. The most consistent verification, however, comes primarily from the sincerity of the author's enthusiasms. Reading *Plenitude* was like being subjected to a 165-page Internet blog composed by one of those latter-day Dr. Strangeloves the Internet is choked with. Whatever else, it wasn't an open "enquiry." Yet it wasn't quite propaganda, or an ideological polemic. Actually, I wasn't sure quite what it was, and that's what disturbed me.

A few years ago, Bosnian playwright Dzevad Karahasan explained Yugoslavia's descent into barbarism by citing a development syndrome that now has global resonance: radical economic and technological openness coupled with cultural and semantic closure. The syndrome is very much a description of the global system over which *Plenitude* drools. The goods get traded, every new technology gets used to full commercial potential, while everyone joins ideological kinship groups and gangs and stops talking about anything that isn't agreeable to the ideological presets or their application manuals.

This is what people like McCracken are now calling "diversity," conflating it (by a spin so blue-eyed optimistic you can feel it spraying white sugar over you) with multiculturalism, the Global Village, and the political condition globalists call post-ideological democracy, which seems to mean laissez-faire capitalism without any noticeable social democratic component. They certainly don't mean biodiversity, and they don't quite mean cultural diversity, even though they'll cheerfully use the latter term interchangeably with what they're really campaigning for: Absolute Entrepreneurial Proliferation.

Besides unleashing or liberating various wealthy spirits from regulatory restraints, Absolute Entrepreneurial Proliferation involves exhorting disbelievers in the Triumph of the Marketplace and other old-fashioned infidels to lose their fears and "embrace diversity." But when it is well-heeled, highly educated art-folks like Grant McCracken exhorting themselves and others to embrace diversity, one can rightfully suspect that the embrace isn't going to be entirely humane. Anyone willing to embrace the ethos evidenced in *Plenitude* will find him or herself wrapped around one of those jumbo shopping carts filled with empty words and intellectual blather, and having a few splendid-looking people of mixed racial backgrounds wearing folk costumes to elite cocktail parties doesn't quite hide the emptiness of it.

Shopping can be great fun, but it shouldn't be mistaken for democracy. Or, as philosopher Joseph Tussman put it in *Obligation and the Body Politic* (1960), "Free men aren't made in supermarkets." We may enjoy increased consumer choices and the mo'big shopping malls, but we've got to be a little cracked if it makes us forget that the contemporary popular culture most fond of diversity's embrace is controlled and shaped by a very small, powerful oligarchy of profit-obsessed corporate managers about as interested in the people's political rights as certain members of the Borgia family were during the Italian Renaissance.

The noise that comes from pumping huge volumes of materiel through a narrow conduit of commerce seems to have convinced McCracken and a lot of other advocates of popular culture that the sludge most people get from the pipe that is perpetually being thrust in their faces is somehow going to liberate the human spirit or save the planet. The true weakness of *Plenitude* is that Grant McCracken doesn't see the pipe at all. Consequently, every hot wank rumbling from the corporations gets used to support his arguments, and if you listen to him too long, it begins to feel like we really are spontaneously speciating and diversifying. This is particularly so if, like McCracken, you happen to believe that the "real" world began around 1975, that whatever happened prior to that is a flat simultaneity one can tamper with to suit one's polemical purposes, and that the contents of the real world are strictly human and technological. Ignore the fading of frog species or the few trillion plankton off the coast of Antarctica that might argue that the increase in diversity and speciation isn't happening. They don't have the language skills McCracken has, and they're not on the cocktail circuit. In the realm of *Plenitude*, if you're not at the party, you don't count.

A related issue I didn't get to — a less serious one — was the incomprehensible blah blah that spewed from *Plenitude* whenever the subject of the Internet was raised. I don't know about you, but I'm really getting tired of hearing how the Internet is about to improve or replace everything from democracy to mucous membrane sexual contact. These are pretty much the same irritating claims techno-enthusiasts were making for artificial intelligence a few years ago. When's the last time you even heard anyone *mention* artificial intelligence?

The reason you don't hear about artificial intelligence is that machine intelligence can't duplicate the contextual leaps organic intelligence routinely makes to parse the simplest metaphor or joke. Except in extremely rare cases, the Internet likewise has produced little more than a lot of self-glamourizing advertorial spam, along with a dim-witted subculture of pixel-drunk zealots armed with a (dare I use the word?) plenitude of half-cooked enthusiasms and ignorant opinions. Rated solely on performance (which the nuclear energy industry should have taught us is a better basis for evaluating high tech than "promise" or other camouflage for manipulated hype), the Internet is now merely an electronic adjunct to the marketplace, not a serious alternative to ground-level political, cultural, and interpersonal cooperation and expression. It ain't going to enhance democracy.

Finally, what I never quite got to say in the original review was that McCracken built his book by ignoring an evident but hard-to-connect truth about our lives that people are increasingly loath to admit. We live as we do because a single instrument — television — which began by threatening to turn us all into conformist automatons, may now have successfully obliterated the possibility of societal coherence and mass commonalities, semantic or otherwise. It, and its technically related antecedents, has achieved this by drenching everything and everyone in an informational cacophony that has changed the strategies by which independent persons comprehend and address the human condition. It forces the individual to make constant public choices about things that are temporal and irrelevant, but which deliver immense riches to remote organizations and suffocate dissent beneath an avalanche of trivial details, subroutines, and data loops.

Our condition as consumers in a depoliticized polis of commercial choices may result in a single political route to the dignity and identity all human beings crave the moment their bellies are full. It will lead us to join exclusionary, hostile subcultures: ethnic groups, preferential minorities, gangs, and mobs. Once inside these subcultures we will hunker down and go to war against all the other ones, all without ever challenging the superimposition of the marketplace, which will cheerfully sell us the weapons and the medical supplies and praise our entrepreneurial elan. Grant McCracken wants us to embrace this as "diversity."

Even if we demur, it is already embracing us. Before too long the ethnically based malls that are already appearing in our larger cities will become ubiquitous, and after that it's a much shorter step than we imagine to ghetto-malls exclusively for, say, the gay community, or malls solely devoted to those obsessed with their bowels so they can get their vitamins, faux organic foods, and high colonics at a single location with underground parking. This may sound sort of charming and harmless until you recognize that malls for people who still read or believe in participatory democracy are a tiny step further, and that their malls aren't going to be the big ones everyone shops at. Once political structure has been wholly supplanted by commercial structure, gang warfare will be universal.

Is it really all this hopeless? No, but we need to take a closer look at what all this techno/human diversification McCracken finds so uplifting actually produces, and what sort of nourishment we're really getting from it. We need to know more than we do about the point at which hors d'oeuvres become potluck, potluck becomes stew, stew becomes gruel or stale leftovers, and so on. Beyond that, we need to remind ourselves of what the superminds of globalist diversity don't like to talk about: that swamp mud is simply biodiversity at the molecular level gone too far.

I don't, meanwhile, recommend that you waste your time reading *Plenitude*, or the volume that has followed it. If you don't want to take my word on this, by all means look it up on the web at www.cultureby.com. There are, in a culture where reading has become a difficult and lonely practice, better books around. Jorge Semprun's *Literature or Life* is now in paperback, if not on the remainder tables, and you could look up Andre Malraux's *Man's Fate* or the later *Man's Hope*. All three of these books will remind you that the only subject that mattered in the twentieth century concerned those points at which radical evil confronted human fraternity — and that in the twenty-first century we're still very much nose to nose with that contrarium, despite the Internet and the creepy embrace of the marketplace and its ersatz diversities. *Plenitude*, meanwhile, is just a fancy word for money and too much time spent nose-to-navel at cocktail parties.

Proofreading Some
War Novels

NEAR THE END OF THE second sentence of the second chapter of
Ernest Hemingway's *A Farewell to Arms* there is an error. It isn't the
five parallel clauses or the convoluted subordinate clauses, which are
accountable to Hemingway's famous "style." The error concerns the
house Lieutenant Henry moves into at Gorizia, which Hemingway
describes as having a wisteria vine "purple on the side of the house."

Lieutenant Henry moved into the house in August, several
months after the spring-blooming wisteria have shed their blossoms.
Wisteria occasionally bloom in mid-to-late summer, but the later
blooms are always sparse, well short of making any vine appear
"purple on the side of the house." The error is egregious for a writer
who made his living as much by attention to details as by anything
the critics ascribed to him, but it is hardly profound, a piece of
authorial carelessness that a New York editor in the 1920s would
hardly be expected to catch. Still, it raised in my mind the question of
how fragile the believability of fiction is, and what creates believability. *A Farewell to Arms*, generally credited as the great American novel
of World War I, gained much of its immediate believability as the
testament of a "Lost Generation" that had fought in and survived
that war. It made me curious to test how well the novel has survived
the passage of time since its publication, and to test it against a more
contemporary novel like Jane Urquhart's *The Stone Carvers*.

I didn't come to rereading Hemingway without preconceptions.
A Farewell to Arms had been almost the last of his work I read. I'd

started with the Michigan fishing stories while I was still in my teens — not a surprising choice for a kid from the wildernesses of northern British Columbia, where being lost was a practical and not a spiritual matter. From those stories I'd gained an appreciation of the recurring character Nick Adams, and I took more of a shine to Hemingway's careful and ritualized approach to fishing and camping than to his notions about terse writing style, which I found kind of corny — pretending to be simple without actually being so.

I'd read most of Hemingway's other work under the influence of Norman Mailer, and given Mailer's proprietary preoccupations — the aftermath of the Second World War, bullfighting schools in downtown New York City, manly behaviours with a more open poke-and-prod orientation than either Hemingway or today's censorious supervisors of correctness will tolerate — it's no surprise I got to *A Farewell to Arms* late. When I did, in 1966, it was in a first-year university English literature class. That's a bad place to get anything straight.

On that first reading I didn't believe much of what I read in *A Farewell to Arms*. The war parts were credible, Lieutenant Henry's easily set-aside pacifism made sense, as did his shooting of a cowardly sergeant during the retreat, which I thought he'd done more out of irritation than a belief in military discipline. I pondered whether I'd have had the jam to jump into the Tagliamento River to avoid being shot, as Lieutenant Henry did, but almost everything else seemed contrived and fatuous: the self-conscious use of parallel clauses to emphasize the collapse of distinction and rank; the Cary Grant (Hallo Daahling!) dialogue between Henry and Catherine Barkley; Henry's deliberately foreshortened perspective and decision-making; and finally, the symbolic symmetry of having Catherine Barkley die in childbirth at the end of the book.

On this reading I understood some of the things I once thought phony with more sympathy, but much of the novel still seemed too cute by a mile. Life is not so simple as to be ordered by sentence structure, and if it is going to resemble a sentence, it will read more like one of Henry James's than Hemingway's. The deus ex machina end to Ms. Barkley rang as falsely as ever, but now I had some inkling about why. Life as we know it today isn't so much a catastrophe as a mess, and doing a walk-through as Lieutenant Henry does, even with the lethal obstructions he faces, doesn't wash. We have to muddle, mess around, without the slightest hope of avoiding responsibility even if the world has ended or is in the process of doing so.

On the positive side, I was pleasantly surprised at how smoothly Hemingway's stylized prose read. From my first reading I recalled how dialogue-heavy the novel was, but now I was impressed by the economy of the descriptive passages, and by the smooth segues in and out of dialogue and description. The self-consciously paralleled sentences were only a minor pain in the ass, and the Barkley/Henry dialogue, which had seemed designed to disclose as little as possible between the two of them, now struck me as sociologically revealing rather than fatuous. The erotic coding hid, given the tenderness of Henry's badly torn-up knee, some of the first blow jobs recorded in an English-language novel. It also occurred to me that a gender-partisan reading would detect the first guys-are-obtuse-dorks novel, because Henry is, in fact, a wonderfully clear illustration of how Western heterosexual males deal — then and now — with love relationships. Henry goes along with Barkley's effusions because he wants to get laid, and then he gets, imperceptibly and without any specific recognition, caught up. Once he does, he plays things as they lay, embracing the same effusion of language he earlier employed for selfish purposes. This reveals the little-recognized truth that dorks play by the rules whether or not they've invented or initiated the game, and that they're surprisingly steadfast about it once they buy in.

Canadian novelist Jane Urquhart's *The Stone Carvers* has an error similar to Hemingway's second-chapter error in its prologue, but it is characteristic rather than egregious. Hemingway knew what a blossoming wisteria looked like trellised across the side of a wall. He simply didn't recall the time of year the vines bloom. Urquhart, by contrast, is characteristically fuzzy about far too many properties of physical life. She thinks there are quintessential Canadian pine trees and appears to believe the same of wildflowers and quite a lot of other things.

There are, for the record, eleven species of native pines growing in different parts of Canada, and several hundred species of wildflowers. Save for similarities in needle and root configuration, the different pines are very different kinds of trees, and the only similarity between our wildflowers is that they grow uncultivated. Equally revealing, Urquhart does not understand that the sounds pine trees make in the wind are not the result of two trees "scraping against each other in a wind-filled Canadian forest" (presumably an archetypical one), but are the acoustical byproducts of small stress fractures within the individual tree trunks that keep them from snapping when the winds reach a reasonable velocity. Where I come from, they're called "tree squeaks" and are famously hunted down by greenhorn woodspersons, and in my experience it is the spruce varieties that most closely replicate the sound of heavy ropes and lanyards banging against stone and other monumental surfaces.

This sort of "quintessentializing" in *The Stone Carvers* — the novel is filled with similarly off-the-mark categorizations — is actually the sound of a novelist working within the confines of a nationalist culture desperate, commercially and otherwise, to distinguish itself from other, larger, same-language juggernauts. As such, some of Urquhart's excesses are forgivable, but they also, almost by themselves, condemn her novel to mediocrity. Only very great writers can make the specific and the archetypical coincide. When they do it successfully — Herman Melville's characterization of the *Pequod*'s first mate Starbuck in *Moby-Dick* is the example that comes to mind — it is usually because they've employed a powerful fastidiousness with the specific. Urquhart is weak on specifics. Her quintessentializing often betrays a dismaying mental laziness, and the truncated research that usually goes along with mental laziness.

I could run the roll on her errors-of-indifferent-research for a very long time, but since Urquhart is a pleasant woman, and most of the goofs she makes are relatively minor — a passage that supposes a round of firewood can be split into four symmetrical pieces with a single blow from an axe, and a more or less complete indifference to which wood species are suitable for carving and what species can go through a sawmill without saw changes, etc. — I'll lay off unless it matters. Unfortunately for someone writing a book about sculpture, Urquhart is a bit of a wood moron. She thinks there are two kinds of wood in Canada: "virgin" trees and "other," which for her are beneath mention. Virginity is a highly desirable Canadian condition for her, and it's hard not to get the impression that she likes both her characters and the forests to be that way whenever possible. Since an official Canadian literature theme is "Loss of Innocence," virgin conditions permit preferred literary drama points. In *The Stone Carvers*, such moments tend to be cataclysmic, a kind of spiritualized falling to the horizontal with a lot of groaning and seemingly painful thrashing and snapping of limbs. By contrast, the sexual encounters in *A Farewell to Arms* read as sanguine and fun-filled — which is a little depressing given what we now know of Hemingway's tortured and prudish ideas about sex.

The Stone Carvers, which is ostensibly about the creation of the memorial commemorating the Canadian military victory at Vimy Ridge in April 1917, is more properly an archetypalizing fantasia of the monument's lineage than a historical dramatization of the events at Vimy Ridge and the building of its memorial. As with most fantasias, it is more interested in celebrating the beliefs and prejudices of contemporary reader-celebrants than in reconstructing history or sorting out its dynamics. *The Stone Carvers*, not surprisingly, coming from a fashionable Canadian novelist, is a *multicultural* fantasia, a kind of puppet show of contemporary Canadian virtues interspersed with flourishes of slightly flushed emotional procurement. The novel is also a pleasant read, if that's all you're looking for, and it is occasionally moving — I found myself in tears several times, particularly while she was describing the Vimy monument itself.

More often on the front burner, alas, was the heavy, emotionalizing hand of the novelist, and misplayed opportunities to actually show us something profound about a profound subject matter. Nothing happens in the book that doesn't directly support

Urquhart's novelistic theme except the obsessive-compulsive obtusenesses of her leading characters attempting to be *deep*. Even the contrived emotional procurements of the characters, elegantly drawn as they often are, seem excessively purposive, and there's a scriptedness that occasionally makes them feel, er, wooden — more like figures in a static tableau than living beings. I'm not asking to see them straining in the washroom or tripping over curbs, just that they be allowed a few of the laughs and pratfalls that keep the rest of us human.

Urquhart's strengths as a novelist are her ability to represent an eccentric delicacy of feeling within the Jane Austen/Virginia Woolf band, and her ability to write elegant if slightly lilac (as Philip Marchand has so deliciously termed it) prose. A multicultural mosaic made up entirely of self-involved obsessive-compulsives might seem a ludicrous (if unintentionally accurate) undertaking, but with an extremely generous suspension of disbelief, Urquhart comes close to making it work. It's only when you begin to scan the rough edges and the mistakes that it falls apart.

The most damning criticisms are that Urquhart doesn't know nearly enough about the Great War to make the book useful as history, and that she's too careless with her details for the book to be educative in any other way. For instance, her understanding of how the battle at Vimy was fought simply isn't adequate.

(1) She thinks the tunnels that released troops close to the German lines were the deciding factor in the Vimy battle. They were contributory but neither unique nor decisive.

(2) She appears to believe that the "rolling barrage" was an innovation first used at Vimy. The Germans had been using it since 1915.

(3) She appears to believe that the "mines" detonated at the beginning of the battle were similar to the land mines of today, when in fact they were much larger, involving underground tunnels dug far below enemy lines, packed with huge volumes of high explosive, and then detonated to destroy or weaken the enemy

bunkers and to kill or disorient the opposing troops at the commencement of combat. Only three of the four mines set to explode at the beginning of the Vimy attack were successfully detonated. (It's also worth mentioning that for obvious reasons there were very few small land mines set by either side during the Great War until the Germans were in full retreat late in 1918.)

(4) She thinks it was the rolling barrage rather than the mine detonations that were heard across the English Channel. It was the detonation of the large mines, but even so, more numerous, larger, and louder mine detonations had been almost a commonplace since early 1916, when the British detonated seven at nearby St. Eloi.

(5) She seems unaware that a twenty-day artillery bombardment preceded the attack, or that roughly 20 percent of the more than one million shells fired didn't explode, thus riddling the Vimy grounds with the unexploded ordnance that remains a hazard to this day.

More generally, Urquhart offers us almost no explanation of why the attack succeeded other than that it had something to do with the "Canadian Character," and she delivers even less concerning the drama of getting the Vimy monument done (as opposed to "sculpted," on which sub-element she's rather good). Its builder, Walter Allward, appears only as a prop for the novel's invented characters: an obsessive-compulsive wood-sculpturing heroine whose emotions are so scarily extreme we're thankful she only experiences them every decade or so; her near-autistic brother who is transformed by his experiences at Vimy (first in 1917, when he loses a leg, and then in 1934, working on the memorial) from a claustrophobic wanderer/hobo to a one-legged homosexual gourmand obsessed with French cuisine; and an Italian-Canadian sculptor who bears a suspicious resemblance to Urquhart's McClelland & Stewart stall-mate Nino Ricci and is obsessed, in a calm, laughing Italian sort of way, with carving people's names in stone.

Allward himself is portrayed merely as a gruffly tolerant paternal eminence. We see nothing to convince us of the enormous ego and will he must have possessed to achieve the preposterous task — pragmatic and bureaucratic — of building the Vimy memorial. Instead we are frog-marched in the direction of a cliché-ridden panorama of today's multiculturalism: Italians who are warm-hearted, hard-working, talkative, and all related to one another (we never find out which part of Italy they hail from); the eccentric German priest who dies as his lifelong obsession with obtaining a bell for his stone church becomes a reality; some stolidly industrious German peasant-technologists; the proto-feminist spinster; the silent-but-poetic Irish lad who abandons everything at the sight of a barnstorming aviator to die anonymously in the muddy trenches and to be memorialized as Canada's unknown soldier by the proto-feminist; the rotund French war veteran and chef whose body is riddled with migrating shrapnel and who emigrates to Montreal with the post-autism one-legged wanderer/hobo protagonist to become a gay restaurateur. I'm grateful that Urquhart stops short of delivering Walkman-toting Somalian or Tamil refugees with hepatitis C and automatic pistols, but by the end of the novel, her relentless attempts to provide full multicultural coverage had grown so oppressive I wouldn't have flinched had she included them in her canvas, too.

The Stone Carvers was published seventy-two years after *A Farewell to Arms*, and so inevitably lacks the authenticating power of personal remembrance and testimony. Yet it seems to me that part of that lost power could have been made up for by more extensive use of the enormous and fully refined factual base that now exists concerning that catastrophe and its aftermath — in which all of us are currently toiling. In the end, Urquhart is content to settle for the idiosyncratic, fancifully following the trail a crazed Bavarian prince (Ludwig the Mad) blazed across a small corner of Canada, and lying low on the infinitely more extensive effect the insanity of another German prince, Kaiser Wilhelm II (along with his differently costumed and equally incompetent colleagues who sat above the opposing trenches sending helpless men to their deaths), had on us. It's a novelist conceit, and her prerogative, I suppose. But had her curiosity been stronger, and her attention to technical detail better, she might have written an important novel instead of yet another supplication to the bullies of contemporary culture. Lilac prose and subtle emotions aren't nearly enough to produce great literature. As with everything else, you have to know the world and its specifics, or at least more than you put on display.

After *Cambodia*

IN 1986 I WROTE *Cambodia: A Book For People Who Find Television Too Slow*. It is now closing in on two decades since its publication, but I've been explaining its unconventional behaviour to readers since the day it appeared. It is a dual-text book with a difference. It doesn't feature two different languages, but a primary text of short philosophical episodes that are printed across the top half of the page, with a book-length essay on Cambodia and related subjects running on the lower half of the page. Conventional literary readers find it confusing to read, and a few, I'm told, simply give up in frustration. But enough other readers have found it cognitively, culturally, and philosophically stimulating — and go on reading with sharper attentions than are usually brought to reading books these days. That's why the book has survived.

Until I wrote *Cambodia* I was a part-time writer of conventional short fiction, and an urban planner with an instinct that nearly all planning problems were actually unrecognized political and cultural problems. I was serious about politics and planning, but I wasn't exactly a full-time serious person. I had an irresistible penchant for sabotaging my co-workers' telephones or the other devices they relied on to keep their sense of self and their grip on reality screwed tight. So I took to unscrewing the bases of their telephones and gluing the handsets to them, or covering the earpieces with shoe polish, or removing the handset microphones so they could only *listen* to incoming calls. All very sophomoric, but a decent antidote to knowing that the work I was being paid for was likely to come to nothing, and that most of the people around me were deluding themselves about what they were doing, and why.

Planning didn't work, and towards the end of my planning career, most of the telephones in the office didn't work. Neither, it seems to me, did conventional fiction, which was and remains almost always about the private epiphanies and humiliations of people so sensitive to themselves that their gaze never quite lifts from their navels to contemplate the human condition in relevant ways. As Cyril Connolly once wrote, neurotics are bores, and I was bored at the thought of spending my life writing about them. Conventional fiction didn't seem an adequate response to a world in which global nuclear winter was only a few insane technical decisions away, in which millions of people had been murdered to protect the purity of harebrained causes and utopian ideas, and where millions more continued to starve or be shot to death each year when the means to prevent it were there if we wanted to use them.

I wanted to write a book that acknowledged the largest and most urgent realities of the world I was in — which in 1986 had had, every day for thirty-five years, fleets of bombers loaded with armed nuclear warheads within a few minutes of the point beyond which there was no way to recall them. The world had also become — and this was important to me as a writer — a place in which everything could be and was communicated, but almost nothing essential to its survival was being seriously discussed. Disturbing to me, writers appeared to be doing nothing to change this. The fiction being written was doing what it had done for most of the century, often elegantly and skillfully, but its range of subject matters was far too narrow, and I could see no way of widening it without tearing its essential culture to pieces. So I decided to write a book by arbitrarily selecting the most difficult subject matter I could locate, and to let that subject matter determine the form its narrative would take.

I didn't embark on this out of a sense of personal disaffection, and I wasn't externalizing any private misery I was harbouring. At the time I was a younger version of what I am today: a perfectly ordinary, blue-eyed, six-foot WASP male, highly domestic, married with three children — two of them now grown — and close to my extended family. I like to cook, I garden in the summers, and I go to the same café every day to work. I've always been, by and large, the sort of person who is physically active and healthy and happy to be alive. I grew up in a small and very rough frontier town in northern British Columbia where I could see what and who was doing what to whom, and why. The code of conduct I grew up with was simple: Die for your friends and family, show no mercy to your enemies, and be polite to strangers. I probably ought to be running a construction company and driving a pickup truck with a rifle on a gun-rack in the back window. But because the world is as open as it is, I've been able to spend my days thinking and writing about the largest and most universal things I can wrap my brain around. I can say, without a trace of irony or cynicism, that this is a wonderful world even if it is filled with horrible things. I think that making the world better and more understandable is the cultural job of writers, and I wouldn't trade my job for anyone's. When I wrote *Cambodia* I was simply learning to take my job seriously where others writers didn't seem willing to.

I chose the subject of Cambodia because I didn't know much about it and dimly understood that my ignorance was shameful. That became the challenge: to erase my ignorance by writing a book that would be determined by the information I gathered and the insights the research engendered rather than by strategy and plan — or by the appropriations of conventional writing skills or genre.

It didn't take long to locate Cambodia — then called Democratic Kampuchea by the Vietnamese-backed successors to the genocidal Pol Pot regime that took over the country at the end of the Vietnam War. In 1986 a few people knew that something terrible had happened in Cambodia, but very few had a clear notion of what it was. This was before the movie *The Killing Fields* was released, and just after William Shawcross's watershed *Sideshow* was published. The Simon Fraser University library, I discovered, had several books and monographs on the subject: Michael Vickery's *Cambodia: 1975–1982*, and a couple of academic monographs by Ben Kiernan that were later published commercially as *How Pol Pot Came To Power* (1985).

But the general subject of what happened to Cambodia and its citizens was of so little public or scholarly interest at the time that none of the books had been catalogued by the university's librarians. A friendly librarian generously gave me access to the uncatalogued books and I wrote letters to Vickery and Kiernan, the latter of whom responded instantly and provided me with a mountain of information he'd gathered, which wasn't available anywhere. So I began my research and quickly tapped into a pipeline of semi-underground materials that all the analysts were completely willing to share.

I discovered that the Khmer Rouge regime of 1975–79, which had been created largely by the trauma of the U.S. Air Force's brutal and illegal carpet-bombing of the country between 1969 and 1973, embarked, once the Americans were gone, on an organized attempt to erase the individual memories and imaginations of Cambodians and to restart the world as a warmed-up Stalinist gulag. Two other things quickly became apparent to me: (1) That the erasure of individual memory and imagination was a recurrent political impulse throughout the twentieth century, and (2) That the mission of television within Western cultures was to accomplish pretty much the same thing.

After about six months of intense and frequently nightmare-invoking research, I wrote the first sentence of the subtext: "We *think* we know what went on in Cambodia ..." — and my world changed forever. The book proceeded by insight rather than by outline. I was trying to find out what was there, and I was willing to follow any associative insight I stumbled onto. For a long time I had no idea what to do with what I was producing. I wrote several of the episodes in the main text and continued with the subtext, drawing from pretty well everything I'd been thinking about since adolescence. I wrote several sections about the history of the Congo all in a swoop because the subject had been on my mind for a long time. There is a poem of mine from the mid 1970s, "The Hand," in the *Oxford Book of Canadian Verse*, which documented the Congo constabulary's practice of accounting for bullets expended with severed human hands, and I'd been puzzling over the meaning of Hannah

Arendt's offhand estimate of "15 to 40 million deaths" there since I read *The Origins of Totalitarianism* in the 1960s.

The illustrative episodes that make up the upper text rapidly accumulated, and the essay on Cambodia grew, but I had no idea how to make a book from it. Eventually, I showed what I had to my editor at Talonbooks, Karl Siegler. He read it through and said, "You have a book here, but it isn't acting like any book I've ever seen. Why don't we run the Cambodia essay underneath the Global Village episodes, because this is a conversation between two subject matters, and they're talking to one another in a unique way. So let's set up the text as a vertical conversation."

That's how the book was built. Karl and I were fitting the parts together, adding clips wherever gaps appeared, right to the day it went to press. One of the things that gave me energy was that the way we were constructing struck me as true to the way we now live and think: fielding information from multiple sources and putting it together in a dynamic matrix that doesn't shape its conclusions before the facts are in. It was true in a way that my previous books weren't. I knew that life no longer has a coherent beginning, middle, and end, so why should the stories and books we write to understand it offer that distorting comfort?

I also liked having a visible and open subtext. It did away with the unacceptable notion that literature is produced for the edification of a literate elite, and that this elite alone fully understands literature — and, by extension, life — because its members are conversant with a set of subtle protocols that underpin human order and action. I'd seen little evidence that either the literate elite or the people — not always the same — who thought they were in charge of the world were aware of *anything* very subtle. Second, I'd had a lifelong dislike of secret societies or anything else that generates insiders and outsiders, maybe because, as someone from working-class hinterland origins, I'd been on the outside watching things malfunction or fall apart under the stress of events.

The presumption that the world operates by secret subtexts and protocols still irritates me. I think that whether they are artistic or political, they merely lend power to oligarchies. Since I object to rule by oligarchy, universally, nationally, or locally, it is my duty to do whatever I can to reveal what they withhold. I also think this is what responsible writers and other artists have done for centuries, and I feel lucky to have stumbled onto a situationally accurate and satisfying way to do my job.

The compositional method I used — and continue to use — carries a heavy debt to computers and word processing, which make it easier to research and write at multiple levels. Similarly, the book's argument with television is not the Luddite argument of one alienated from either the sharp edges of technology or the medium's enticements. It embraces useful technology and acknowledges the power of television. Electronic information technologies have created two main effects. The first is to create a metaphor — the Global Village — that implies the existence of planetary communal experience, but in reality merely delivers the technical framework for commercial exploitation of it. The second effect, more technical and less recognized or studied, is the emergence of a virtual simultaneity of history and binary-formatted information (including television) that has convulsed human cognition for the last forty years. We can theoretically know everything, but are subtly encouraged to know nothing, to give up understanding to play within a technologically enhanced sensorium.

Television has been the primary instrument of communalization. Because it compresses and summarizes the world and then funnels it through the narrow conduit of low-density pixel matrices, television appears to be increasing the flow of information and increasing its velocity. But the information we get from it is simplified, cluttered with commercial submessages, and further slowed by the technical limitations of the medium, which, to hold viewers' attentions, overuses dramatic spectacle and simple-minded storylines. There's also an ideological (and, one suspects, economic) prejudice built into television: that people are fundamentally stupid. The result is an outpouring of information that has the appearance of speed and completeness, but is actually low-grade narrative gruel in which the hidden storyline is always the same: Buy more, think less. This is the dark side of Marshall McLuhan's famous remark that "the medium is the message." He was right. The primary content of television is television itself. The secondary content is determined by the owner-operators.

Binary technology has liberated the human mind and alienated it at the same time. Television, computers, and all digital technologies operate by lateral yes/no decisions at a speed 2.4 million times faster than neural synapses travel within human nerve tissue. This has freed a small percentage of us from routinized mental and productive tasks, and that is to the good. But the cognitive architecture and operational logic of a computer are easily mapped and reproduced. The architecture and operating system of the human brain remain, by contrast, a matter of speculation. In the absence of a clear understanding of how human intelligence works, we have been unable to draw binary technologies into a human and humane context.

This is a dangerous state of affairs because binary technology has intelligence, and it is imposing it on us. As binary technologies become more powerful, they are eroding our ability to contextualize the multiplying environments within which we operate. We have been losing context for forty years, and television has been, so far, the chief culprit. We produce more reporting of events, more dramatic fictions, and more simulations of phenomena, but we have failed miserably to contextualize any of it, or to model a verticality of perception that enables the complex sense of perspective that is our natural ability and our antidote to binary logic and production.

Human and binary intelligence aren't a good fit. Numbers and experience, in isolation from one another, tend to twist and then totalize human understanding. Human intelligence naturally invites us to draw the connections between numbers and personal experience, a procedure that slows or arrests binary — and dialectical — reasoning processes, and leads us away from them, and away from totalities of any kind. Totalitarianism isn't a coherent or complete system of human relations, just as capitalism isn't. Both are like a car that has an engine but no transmission. You sit in the driver's seat, step on the gas, and it makes a lot of noise and burns a lot of resources and makes you feel warm — and then the motor blows up and sets fire to the vehicle. When you're in the middle of history and time, it is easy to lose track of the fact that the motors are purring away, but that you're not getting anywhere and the motors are over-heating.

Democracy is the only complete system of human relations ever invented — inefficient and incoherent as it is — because it demands that citizens know where they are and why, and because it generates feedback and understanding, whether or not citizens pay much attention to it. Democracy is thus dynamic and capable of self-correction, whereas authoritarian systems are not and can be changed only by violence to the system. We haven't managed to come up with an economic system that works yet, which is why we're destroying the planet we live on.

It is the gift and the curse of the human brain, which cybernetic theoreticians describe as a fully integrated neural network and which thus operates on a radically different basis than a computer or a television set, that it insists on perspective, coherence, context — however partial or confused. The result of our current failure to pay attention to perspective and context is a billion consciousnesses that are falling into non-contextualizing coherences — the fake communality of the Global Village — which turn people to the pursuit of binary purities and mutually isolated universes that don't connect one to another in any meaningful way. It may be transforming us into a vast tribe of self-determining monomaniacs cohabiting primarily with the technologies around them and wishing to live in self-contained monocultural utopias — little Cambodias — that could, as our raw materials dwindle, make Pol Pot's nightmare of repression and violence seem like an amusement park.

It is this oncoming nightmare that I discovered with *Cambodia: A Book For People Who Find Television Too Slow* and then developed further with *Public Eye: An Investigation into the Disappearance of the World*, which was published in 1989. Both are attempts to reinvent a formal verticality of perception within what I'm fully aware is an obsolete medium — the printed book. Their discursive method is presentational and provisional rather than conclusive. Both books are filled with laughter. That laughter is deliberate. Laughter, neurologically, is the sole offensive weapon that contextual and vertical thinking have against the calculative power of binary logic and its devices. Laughter disrupts logic, and it is no accident that the sole trait that is universal to all human cultures is the appetite for slapstick. This appetite likely saved more lives than penicillin in the twentieth century. Given the number of people who lost their lives, it hasn't been very effective. But it is all we have.

It has been pointed out to me that I'm not the first Canadian to track these sorts of issues. Harold Innis pioneered the sociological study of communications in the 1940s until his death in 1953, and Marshall McLuhan redeployed many of Innis's insights as the basis for his own analyses of mass communications. Why Canada, a nation of 30 million people stretched across the widest range of geographies on the planet, and with the most culturally diverse citizenship, is so interested in the dynamics of mass communications is a question worth asking. The standard answer is that in a country so physically vast and sparsely populated we need to be focused on how well we communicate with one another or the country will fall apart. But I think it has more to do with being a mouse living next door to an elephant — the United States, with all its imperial pretensions and cultural force — that makes us acutely aware of such issues. If we're not wary and resourceful, the elephant will step on us. So Canadians pay attention to large systems, and we critique the world-according-to-the-U.S. with special care. It's not enough for Canadians to be who we are. We have to be aware of why we're different from Americans, and why we don't want to be Americans, because if we don't, we're going to *be* Americans. Very poor, second-class ones. The continued existence of authentic Canadian culture is an astonishing accomplishment given the power of globalism and the immense reach of American cultural products.

Cambodia is often described as a prehistory of globalization, but *Public Eye* is more accurately that because it was focused on the economic and neurological phenomena that global systems have imposed on the human community. *Cambodia* was my recognition that we were living in a different world than the one most people thought they were in, and a warning that the Global Village was marginalizing more people than it would liberate. After all these years, the book seems prescient beyond both my wildest hopes and worst nightmares.

Writers and Responsibility

A COUPLE OF YEARS AGO the editor of the Writers' Union of Canada newsletter asked me to comment on whether writers needed to be concerned about the social effects of their work. My first response was that there's madness afoot when supposedly serious people aren't sure of the answers to such questions. This one raised the horrifying possibility that some writers today are wondering if they still need to be concerned about the social (and I assume that includes political, cultural, and expressional) effects of what they write, and of writing in general.

So there's no confusion about what I think, my answer to this question is an emphatic yes. Writing should be aimed at having an effect on the culture and politics of the society from which it comes. At the most general level, a writer's job is to make life better, or at least more intelligent and informed. But let me turn the question slightly, and then break it down. Shouldn't writers today be concerned that our work has little or no effect? Has our sheltered status turned us into such weenies that we've come to believe in the helium-infused *infra dig* of contemporary formalist art, and do we suppose that the triumph of the marketplace has freed us of all responsibilities except the need to be productive and profitable producers and marketers? Are writers buying into a view so dislocated from civil responsibility that when almost no one gives a damn about what writers think and write, we mistake it for freedom of speech? Is political and cultural indifference to art a freedom we want?

I don't think any of these questions are rhetorical, and that's a depressing reflection of how far the philosophical bulldozing by the marketplace has penetrated civil and cultural activities. Two decades ago, none of these questions would have been taken seriously because nearly all writers would have instantly answered "yes" to the initial question — and then scoffed at the asker. Just the fact that asking the other questions seems necessary tells me how much things have changed. Writers have lost to television most of the cultural influence they once took for granted, while books, except maybe for novels, have lost their cachet in the marketplace. That's why writers — or organizations like the Writers' Union — spend most of their energy fussing over which asses their members should be looking to kiss in order to make a decent living and/or avoid complete irrelevance.

It gets more depressing. The Writers' Union question was in code. Hidden in it was this question, engineered from multicultural terror and the presence of too many children's writers and writers of young adult fiction: Should the work of today's writers contain unfashionable ideas and characters — like, say, a loud-talking, bum-pinching, sexist business jerk who wants to put an end to government subsidies — when there's the possibility that impressionable high-school students might take him for a role model? They were asking, in other words, if writers should censor themselves before the fact to ensure that they don't offend a newly offence-alert society.

There's a simple, direct answer to that one, too: No. Most writers are already censoring themselves as they scour the marketplace for a potentially marketable whiff of the new *Zeitgeist*. The equally scary corollary is that many writers think this question has just been invented.

In a democracy, freedom of expression and speech are, theoretically, rights that writers must defend at any and all cost, both as citizens and artists. Here in Canada we haven't had much occasion to defend those rights, unless we've been clumsy (or foolish) enough to insult the aggressively tender sensibilities of Islam, our racial minorities, or Conrad Black. Canadian writers have had it so easy, actually, that they've forgotten that writing directly and openly about what's on one's mind used to be dangerous, and still is in many parts of the world. They've also, methinks, largely forgotten that 99 percent of the books worth reading over the centuries became worthwhile because their authors risked that danger. That we're asking ourselves whether writing is worth the risk demonstrates the degree to which today's writers have already come to think of themselves as mini-factories for the entertainment industry, or as proactive practitioners of the general right of therapeutic self-expression.

Our democratic tradition also confers two duties that most writers in Canada seem to have forgotten. One of them is the duty to seek out and speak — accurately and in detail — that which is not being spoken of. In Canada, as in most of the Western democracies, that used to be sex and gender, but it is now more likely to be social democracy or the unearned privileges of the corporations. The other duty, interestingly, qualifies speaking the unspeakable as an act of civilized behaviour. It is the duty of discretion, from which we are never free, and shouldn't be. Discretion is an immensely complicated duty to practise accurately because it requires us not only to know and present the accurate details, but also to understand who we are and what we wish to speak and write about, along with the location and sensitivity of the blameless. These are as much political duties, by the way, as artistic ones.

For several decades, Canadian writers, encouraged by relatively generous cultural subsidies, have busied themselves with creating a national literature that gives expression to the increasingly complex diversities of life within our borders. It's been a unique project, and we've acted as a kind of national defence corps of the mind. Speaking the unspeakable has been part of this, but in recent years the speaking has been rather muted unless we are trying to normalize the unconventional side of our individual identities. Today it feels like writers are less a defence corps and more a police force or cheerleading contingent for ascendant prejudices.

I'm suggesting that the new arena of the unspeakable is located in the general area of the marketplace rather than amongst our individual and subcollective social, sexual, and cultural behaviours. In future, we may want to write about the things that Canadians share, and be a little more critical about all those uniquenesses that separate us from one another. I hope we can rediscover discretion and courage along the way, and leave censorship to the busybodies, police work to the justice system.

Cosmopolitans and the Definition of 'Good Family'

I FIRST MET PATWANT SINGH a few years ago during a luncheon at a Toronto movie-star hangout, Joso's. At the time, I'd never heard of him and had to be dragooned into going by writer Nazneen Sheikh. She said he'd be worth my while — and then admitted that she wanted me there to add balance to what she claimed would otherwise be a bunch of extremely bright and talented women writers drooling over an elderly Sikh intellectual.

That was intriguing, because it sounded like I was being invited to serve as ballast, not to add balance. Neither is a role I play often, but I agreed to go anyway — I owed her a favour. Much of my reserve about it derived from the dim view I had of Sikhs. I'd spent years living in Vancouver, where the city's sizable Sikh population has tended to be overly aggressive — economically and sometimes physically — and interested, as far as I could see, in little else than other Sikhs and the ongoing wrangle over how to achieve an independent political state — Khalistan — within India's Punjab region. The only time I'd had extensive contact with a Sikh individual was while I was teaching university courses in the federal prison system in B.C. One of the students was a Sikh in his late twenties who'd been convicted of a grisly double murder, one committed with a bread-knife and the other, reputedly, by squeezing the victim's head in a vise. The student was pleasant enough in class, but the details of his trial defence were off-putting. Among other things, he'd claimed that the bread-knife murder weapon was part of his religious paraphernalia, the *kirpan*, which is a short sword worn for ceremonial purposes. I never heard the religious rationale for the vise, but it smacked of sadism or, worse, torture. I didn't ask him to elaborate on any of it.

So I showed up for the luncheon late, and then mostly because Nazneen's track record for these sorts of events has been extremely reliable. Whatever I might think of Patwant Singh, I decided, I wasn't likely to be bored. What I found at Joso's was an older but not elderly man of medium height, elegantly dressed, and coiffed in a navy blue turban. He was surrounded, as advertised, by a collection of Canada's most high-powered women writers. They were hanging on his every word and otherwise behaving like Valley girls who'd just cornered a rock star. My arrival barely elicited a glance, and then only from Nazneen, who graciously gave up her seat next to the star to allow me to catch the show at ringside.

I listened. Patwant is a spellbinding conversationalist, but this wasn't small talk he was offering, or mere charm. He was delivering the world — large and cosmopolitan. I listened for three hours, as raptly as the others if not quite for the same reasons. And then I did something I've never done in my life, before or since. I asked a stranger for the meaning of life.

Patwant didn't flinch, nor did he seem particularly surprised that I'd asked. He considered my question for a moment, then answered it. "Live without fear or rancour," he said. After another brief pause, he added, "And come from a good family."

I understood the first part of his answer. I'd already gathered — since richly confirmed — that this is how he lives. It can mean jumping off the end of a dock in Finland, turban and all, with a group of Scandinavian diplomats a few days before the late-October ice floes lock in place, or it can mean speaking his mind about politics and religious culture inside a country — India — where to do so as clearly as he does involves risking one's life. You live this way, he explained, because if you don't, you have no life worth living. If your actions and your words are free of rancour and envy, you assure yourself of the good will of all decent men and women. That is as much as you should ask of others.

The second part of his answer was slightly disappointing. Patwant is a well-educated and independently wealthy Indian. Was he merely referring to an Indian version of noblesse oblige, the obligation of wealth and privilege that some — increasingly few — well-off people accept and practise? For me, that wasn't helpful, and, in a way, was not even understandable. I'm a middle-class North American from working-class immigrant origins. My family has little sense of history and tradition. Its notions of human solidarity are rudimentary, reach back barely a generation, and carry no sense of social obligation that isn't self-promotional or expedient. I have no strong sense of whether my family is a good one or not, and no preconceived — or received — notion of what a "good" family ought to be and do for its offspring. For sure, my family provided me with some strengths — it raised me as a mammal with a conscience — but it was and remains, as families go, far more focused on increasing its private wealth than on liberal education, public well-being, or community responsibility. Could Patwant have meant that a large part of living a worthwhile life simply involved how you manipulated the silver spoon someone else put in your mouth? If so, that was troubling, because my silver spoon just isn't very big, and it contains so little precious metal I'd be hard-pressed to fill a dental cavity.

Over the last few years I've seen Patwant several more times because he visits Canada more or less annually. I'm not quite on the A-list for his visits, but I'm grateful for what I get. At one dinner party a year or so after the Joso's event, I got to spend an entire evening watching Margaret Atwood placing intellectual volleyballs above the net for Patwant to spike. He nailed every one, but I left unsure whether Patwant's performance or the sight of Canada's most famous writer cheerfully playing his straight man was the more remarkable. Since I'd seen Patwant's intellectual daring and elegance before, I decided that Atwood's admirably ego-free performance was the greater one. I realize I may be making Patwant sound like Hanif Kureishi's Buddha of Suburbia, but he's a lot more than merely another visiting fakir flogging mental gimmicks and exercise plans. Canada is part of the world he inhabits.

I've also now read four or five of Patwant's books, at least two of which, *Of Dreams and Demons* and *The Sikhs*, are available in North

America and deserve a much wider audience than they've achieved. *Of Dreams and Demons* is an intellectual memoir in which Patwant proves to be far more interested in the swirl of India's history and politics than in himself. It is also the best primer available on the dangers India faces from the Bharatiya Janata Party (BJP), the Hindu chauvinist political party that has been ascendant since the collapse of the Congress Party and that is currently threatening to turn India into a theocracy. *The Sikhs* is a polemical history of India's 20 million Sikhs that, among other things, exposed most of what I thought I knew about Sikhism as an ill-informed misreading.

Patwant's writing has qualities I've come to think of as character-istically South Asian — in other words, he doesn't write sentences like Hemingway. Rather, his prose often borders on the prolix and the symphonic, as if the English language were an instrument best played flamboyantly. Salman Rushdie's best work has this quality, as does some of Amitav Ghosh's. Among journeyman South Asian writers this can result in an irritating wordiness and in novels that double as doorstops. But in Patwant's hands, startling things hap-pen, as in this passage from his introduction to *The Sikhs*:

It is argued in favour [of the caste system] that despite the multiplicity of cultures and communities, and the many ideological challenges it has faced, India has "produced a high degree of ideological tolerance and flexibility." Not really. Because institutionally "Indian society has been traditionally very rigid, working out a precise and clearly identifiable hierarchy, formalized rules, and conventions, conformity with which was mandatory and defined by birth, and a system of substantive and symbolic distances which articulated the hierarchy in a definitive and predictable manner." In the end, India was landed with "a kind of tolerance" which is "only another name for intolerance, namely tolerance of injustice and disparities and of humiliation and deprivation by superior individ-uals and groups." This is what the caste system has been about over the centuries.

The understated incisiveness of that "Not really" lodged between the opposing quotes is a marker typical of his scholarly surety as well as his intellectual style. It comes, I suspect, from not being fearful of rocks and hard places, and of making swift judgments without rancour. He is a living reminder that the social purpose of an intellectual is not to keep order but to point to what is true and to uncover half-truths and outright lies. Which brings me back to what Patwant really meant by "come from a good family."

Patwant Singh is a cosmopolitan, and he is a Sikh. No, these are not contradictory. Sikhdom — or Sikhism — is neither purely a religion nor a territorially based political movement but a civil philosophy. That it has evolved into a religion and a periodically insurgent political movement in response to the conditions it has met is, in an important respect, a diminution. It arose in the late fifteenth century in reaction to the failure of the two world religions of the Indian subcontinent, Hinduism and Islam, to be politically and morally just. The life of Sikhism's first guru, Nanak (1469–1539), is almost exactly coincident with that of Martin Luther (1483–1546), who nailed his ninety-five theses to the door of the church in Wittenberg because the Roman Catholic apparatus of Christianity had similarly failed to be politically and morally just.

In a way, therefore, the Sikhs are best understood by Westerners as the Protestants of the Indian subcontinent. The physical conditions that created them are local — the Punjab region lies along the border between Hindu India and Islamic Pakistan, and it, along with the Sikhs, has been a provocation and a prize to both religions for four hundred years. Yet its spiritual and political dissidence resemble that which existed in fifteenth-century Europe, and the subsequent internal breaches between philosophical intent and political practice that have occurred among Christian Protestants and Sikhs are largely accountable to local physical conditions and the threats each movement faced within the larger histories of Europe and northwestern India.

Sikhism begins as a rejection of the Hindu caste system, seeking to combine the inherent compassion at the root of Hinduism with Islam's concept of equality in the sight of God. The 974 hymns attributed to guru Nanak reject the doctrine of predestination that is at the root of the Hindu caste system, along with the strains of sectarian absolutism that run through Islam. Many of the early Sikh hymns are startlingly declarative and clear: "There is no Hindu, there is no Mussalman" or "If you believe in pollution at birth, there is pollution everywhere." Whatever excesses Sikhism's radical edge has led its adherents to in the distant and more recent past — and these are all our media systems make visible, as with any other culture or religion — it is a philosophy and a culture aimed at balance between the temporal and the spiritual (*meeri* and *peeri*), and between Islam and Hinduism.

There are some curious parallels between the situation of the Sikhs today and Canada's position between the Soviet Union and the U.S. during the Cold War. Among the more damaging possibilities Canada had to endure was the thirty-year psychic threat of a sky filled with crossing nuclear missiles a few moments before Armageddon and nuclear winter. The Sikhs now face something similar if India and Pakistan end up in a nuclear duel, because the Punjab will be one of the primary battlegrounds, and its population will be among the first casualties. The difference between Sikh culture and Canada is that the Sikhs have been physically embattled almost from the beginning, and the kinds of threats they have confronted over the last four hundred years have been vastly more material and constant than anything Canada has faced in its attempts to forge a political and cultural path that is neither American nor European. This has made the best Sikhs into reluctant warriors. Canada's experience, particularly in this century, has turned its best into demoralized peacemakers who don't quite believe that peace is possible. There are things Canadians could learn from the Sikhs, just as there are things that could be learned by returning to Martin Luther and rediscovering what it was that so angered him. We would find, in both cases, people facing cultural and political monoliths willing to commit any *Realpolitik* excess necessary to freeze the status quo and serve the interests of the elite. The exercise might be salutary.

Which brings me again to what it was Patwant meant by "coming from a good family." When the tenth guru of Sikhism, Gobind Singh, baptized five men into the brotherhood of the Khalsa in March 1699 — on the anniversary of Gautama Buddha's enlightenment — the men were not related biologically, nor were they aristocrats. They were five men of different caste and geographical origins, united by their courage and character within what was intended to be a "casteless community of inspired people." After Gobind baptized the five, he was in turn baptized by them as an equal. The virtues the baptism counselled were the virtues that Patwant himself possesses and practises — namely, fearless, rancourless belief in the essential equality of human beings and the moral imperative to do something about making that belief a reality. That makes his "good family" possible — if very difficult — to join.

This may sound like I'm about to join the Sikh religion. I'm not. Patwant Singh is an interesting and intelligent man, and he comes, as he says, from a good family. But it isn't his turban that makes this so. That's of no more fundamental importance than Che Guevara's red star or Osama bin Laden's scimitar and brandished Koran. Do all religions turn parochial? Almost invariably. Only because of pressures from outside? Not necessarily. Fundamentalist Jews thought up their wackiness all on their own, without help from Nazis or Palestinians. And the same can be said for other religions that began as civil philosophies — most glaringly, Marxism.

The litmus tests are the propensity to turn doctrinaire and puritanical, and the ability to retain a sense of humour. The latter of those is, in my mind, the defining plurality that every civil philosophy seems to lose when it turns into religion or partisan politics. Sikhism began as a civil philosophy, as a response to the failure of religion to translate into civilities people can live meaningful lives with. Then it got twisted by four hundred years of violence at the hands of Islam, Hinduism, and (arguably least but not inconsequentially) British imperialism. Are those metamorphoses inevitable? I don't know. But if they are, the human species is probably doomed.

The point I want to make is not that Patwant Singh or Sikhism is the answer, but that Patwant's cosmopolitan stance is the beginning of an answer. Throughout this book (and for most of my adult life) I've argued that the other parts of the answer to the human condition are critical education, laughter, and attention to specificity and particularity — local matters — because these are the grounds that keep cosmopolitan civil philosophies from the religious idiocies and political violence that are always pushing against their boundaries. The commies, during their heyday, were perceptive enough to recognize that this sort of radical cosmopolitanism was a serious threat. That's why they accused their intellectual dissidents of being "rootless cosmopolitans."

To be accurately cosmopolitan is to be virtually the opposite of rootless. Patwant Singh's cosmopolitanism is rooted not merely in his Sikh heritage, but in the things Sikhism tried to claim as the basis for civil harmony: temporal accuracy and the individual dignity that comes from its practice, the need for social and political justice, and the desire to live without fear and without rancour.

I can't think of anything more worthwhile to do with a life, be it individual or collective. Or anything more difficult to achieve. But at least the attempt won't land me, homeless and alienated, at globalism's world mall, which is where we'll all be living if we don't learn new ways to exercise our faculties.

Index